Samuel Kettlewell

The Three Venerable Ladies of England on Church Politics

Madam Britannia, Mother Church, and the Old Lady in Threadneedle Street

Samuel Kettlewell

The Three Venerable Ladies of England on Church Politics

Madam Britannia, Mother Church, and the Old Lady in Threadneedle Street

ISBN/EAN: 9783337077143

Printed in Europe, USA, Canada, Australia, Japan

Cover: Foto ©ninafisch / pixelio.de

More available books at **www.hansebooks.com**

Ex Libris
C. K. OGDEN

THE

Three Venerable Ladies of England,

ON

CHURCH POLITICS.

MADAM BRITANNIA, MOTHER CHURCH,

AND THE OLD LADY IN THREADNEEDLE STREET.

BY THE

REV. S. KETTLEWELL, M.A.

Author of "The Rights and Liberties of the Church;"
"The Reformation in Ireland," etc.

LONDON:
W. SKEFFINGTON, 163, PICCADILLY;
SIMPKIN, MARSHALL, & Co.
1874.

PREFACE.

Matters concerning the interests of the Church are now so freely discussed in public, and will probably, sooner or later, come to the front in our Legislative Assemblies that more thorough and fuller information seems called for respecting them than can be given in the small compass of a short paper or article. Something more than a general view, or discussion of these matters is needed. And there are two or three things, at the present time, which make it the more important to give a somewhat exact and evidential account of them. These are, the more extended and better Education which is given to the people—the great extension of the Franchise of late years—and the recent attempts which have been made to poison the Public mind against the Church and her interests.

Although a certain number of persons will still be led away by the clap-trap oratory of designing men, and be misled by the false or distorted views and statements of unscrupulous zealots, who begrudge the Church her position and possessions,—the number of persons who will begin to think, and determine, and act for themselves in England will increase more and more. Hence appears the necessity of promptly exposing and refuting the fallacies of those who would impose upon their credulity, and of affording them every opportunity of judging for themselves about the truth, and fairness, and justice, of the matters under discussion; so that they may themselves in some degree decide upon the merits of them, rather than take the *ipse dixit*, or follow the lead, of some wily politician or sectarian, who has not himself, it may be, looked fully or accurately into these questions, and but imperfectly understands their bearing upon the public welfare.

Great efforts, then, should be made at the present time to inform the Public mind on these points,—by a plain and faithful account of such matters respecting the interests of the Church which are called in question,—by shewing the justice of her cause,—the reason for upholding her,—and by giving sufficient evidence as to the truth and fairness of what has been advanced in her behalf. And we doubt not but that these efforts will bear fruit, and, that in the majority of cases where the people have the opportunity of fully considering these questions for themselves, a right decision will be come to in favour of the Church. The Church has nothing to fear, but will gain much by the spread of information, and the search after truth in things that concern her welfare. This is the object of the following pages. Especial attention has been given to shew that the Revenues of the Church, of which certain persons are anxious to deprive her, *are the accumulations* of the Voluntary system which has existed for ages past in the Church. And whilst urging forward a resolute and continued defence of the Church,—exposing and refuting the errors and misrepresentations of her adversaries as we have gone along—we have advocated as of supreme moment, the desirability of the Church having the free exercise of her Rights, as other religious Bodies have. The union of Church and State must still be maintained, but in a different, though not less efficient manner. This free exercise of Rights by the Church whilst in entire Union with the State we have made a point of contending for in these pages, as well as elsewhere, as both essentially practical and advantageous to both Church and State, and as more in keeping with the spirit and principles of civil and religious Liberty, and of the British Constitution, than the withholding of them.

Whilst the State or Government should courageously and honestly protect the property of the Church from waste or robbery, be it either from within or from without, we maintain that it should give every facility to the exercise of her just Rights as can be consistent with good order and her real welfare ;—not cutting her adrift as in the case of the Church of Ireland, but still retaining a supreme control over her—as a temporal ruler;—a control to be carefully and lawfully exercised in cases of need;—guiding and assisting her meanwhile to a proper and efficient exercise of her Rights.

A popular form of setting forth these matters has been adopted, as most calculated to engage the generality of minds, and enable them more easily to grasp and comprehend them. Respecting the personages who are supposed to hold conversation together,—Mother Church is, of course, to represent the Church of England and speaking on her behalf,—the Old Lady from Threadneedle Street, her friend, as the representative of the wealth and property of the Kingdom,—and Madam Britannia as the representative of temporal power and authority. John Bull is brought in, but not prominently, as speaking for the people.

HEMEL HEMPSTEAD,
1874.

CONTENTS OF PARTS.

I.

Mother Church's trouble.—The occasion of her visit to the Old Lady in Threadneedle Street.—The design to rob the Church of her possessions talked over.—The Advice of the Lady in Threadneedle Street.—An Anecdote of her early history.—The Defence of the Church must be resolute and thorough.—Disendowment disastrous.—How the poor would suffer most.—The wide-spread value of the Church's System.—The State alone not able to carry it out.—Danger of suffering the people to be deluded.—They should be kept well informed of the truth respecting Church affairs.—The Restoration of the Rights and Liberties of the Church necessary for her proper defence.—How this is to be attained.—An interview with Madam Britannia suggested.

II.

Mother Church's visit to Madam Britannia,—Mr. Bull also introduced.—Both persons interested in averting the threatened spoliation of the Church.—Mr. Bull forewarned of the Stratagem to mislead him.—Church property not National property apart from the Church.—A short sketch of the way in which the Property of the Church was acquired and secured to her.—The sad results that would arise from spoliation.—The Church has a right to be fairly dealt with in all Constitutional changes.—She should be put into the way of managing her own affairs, and governing herself.—Eight Particulars thereof enumerated.—How the Supremacy of the Crown and Civil authority must still be upheld.—The creation of more Dioceses advocated.—All reasonable demands should be persevered in.

III.

All the Three Ladies meet in Conference.—Redress is open to all in the State, but not for imaginary grievances to the hurt of others.—Further Misrepresentations about Church Property confuted.—Church Property not given by the Nation.—How it can never be National Property except through the ministrations of the Church.—It cannot be alienated by Parliament without violating the first principles of right and justice. - Civil Enactments were made to uphold the just claims of the Church.—Payments are to be enforced by Law, as any other claims, because justly due. - The Fallacy of some Popular notions.—The Church of England does not include the whole of the People.—Nor is it confined only to the Clergy, but includes the Lay-members.—The design of Corporations Sole and Aggregate to preserve the property in perpetuity to the Church.

IV.

Some objections of the enemies of the Church to her retaining her Endowments considered and refuted.—The Church's Title to property compared with other Titles.—The Sources from which she obtains Proofs of her Title.—Terriers—Parochial and Diocesan Registers,—as well as by Prescription and Ancient Documents.—Endowments originated in Voluntary gifts.—Evidences from "Newcourt's Repertorium."—Old Records of Gifts to the Church.—The Monasteries in Anglo-Saxon times the Homes of the Evangelizing Clergy, and under the Bishops.—Evidence from the Doomsday-Book to the Church's owning much property.—Also from a letter of William the Conqueror. -- A Deed of Gift to Westminster Abbey, an example of a multiplicity of other gifts.—The Church of England in no wise indebted to the Church of Rome for her Endowments. - The Ancient Sees and Monasteries endowed before the Church of Rome gained her great power in this Country.—The Church of Rome fleeced the Church of England.

V.

The Right of the Church to *Tithes* considered.—How doubts about this have been raised by the enemies of the Church. -- Their Objections and Errors considered and refuted. --Misrepresentations of Mr. Miall.—His indebtedness to Selden and others, whose words he often perverts. -Some account of Selden's work on Tithes.—Mr. Miall's statement that Three-fourths of the Parochial Endowments of the Church were given by Act of Parliament in Edward VI.'s reign proved to be utterly false.—This was a time when the Church was largely fleeced.- How Errors and Misrepresentations are propagated.—The History of Tithes given.—Ethelwulf's Charter considered.—Offa's Law.—Tithes firmly settled by the Laws of the Realm.- Proofs of Tithes being due to the Church before these Laws were made. — How the Church became entitled to them.—The Right of the Church to them proved.

VI.

Collateral Evidence relative to the voluntary origin of Tithes, in the Unequal size of Parishes and the Amount of Tithes, and in the existence of Private Patronage. — Affirmed by Soames and Selden.—Legislative enactments respecting Tithes in Anglo-Saxon times,—at the Norman Conquest and afterwards,— and at the Reformation and afterwards.—A summing up of the arguments and evidences in favour of the Right of the Church to Tithes.—Dissenters would be zealous upholders of the Tithes, did they belong to them.--See what the Puritans did.—Testimony of honest Dissenters to the Church's Right to them.—Recent Church Endowments.- Loose notions as to their security condemned.—The amount of Voluntary Contributions in the Church very large.—Security of all Endowments necessary to encourage liberal gifts.—The Duty of the State to secure the Church's Right to her property.—How the State neglects its duty, and abuses its power if it does not. - The proper Function of the State as to the Rights of all subjects.— The various Rights of the Church should be freely exercised, even whilst in Union with the State; being more consistent with the Spirit and Principles of the British Constitution.—How the Scandal of Selling Church Livings may be remedied.

THE THREE VENERABLE LADIES OF ENGLAND, ON MATTERS CONCERNING CHURCH AND STATE.

MOTHER CHURCH had been much annoyed of late, and her usual equanimity had been greatly disturbed by the inroads which had been made upon, what she had regarded as, her prerogatives, and by the rumour of attempts that would be made to deprive her of her property. Generally she pursued the even tenor of her way,—quietly minding her own duties, and leaving other people to attend to theirs. She had been more active too of late—getting through much more work, and being more successful in her operations than usual; but other people would not let her alone,—they would always be meddling with her affairs. And whether they did not like to see her so busy, and were jealous and envious of her prosperity or no, there had been latterly a number of restless, dissatisfied persons, going about the country, stirring up men's minds against her. They said they wanted to do her good; to give her more liberty, and help her to better herself; but she knew they meant no good in the end: that their shew of good-will was but a pretence to deceive people; that their real design was to do her harm, and to raise up such an agitation in the country about her, that Parliament might be induced, under the cover of granting her more freedom, to despoil her of her possessions, and turn her out into the world as a pauper, to beg for her living. This of course caused her no little uneasiness; and she determined to consult an old friend, with whom she had formerly been intimate, —who was a shrewd observer, and knew the ways of the world better than she did;—and so talk the matter over with her.

Now, this friend, to whose place Mother Church made her way, was an old Lady living in Threadneedle Street. And on this particular morning the Lady had been busy as usual, seeing the heads of the different departments of her large establishment;—consulting with some about matters which required consideration, and giving various orders to others. And now, having settled her affairs, and arranged her sundry papers, she had reseated herself at her desk-table, and had just re-adjusted her spectacles ; and was preparing herself to enjoy a few quiet moments of retrospection and prospection ;—for she liked calmly to consider the steps she had taken, that they were satisfactory ; and still more so, to look a little a-head of things,—to provide against contingencies ; and to see what line of conduct she must take, and what orders she must give for the future so as to advantage her establishment. She had just re-seated herself, I say, and re-adjusted her spectacles, when one of her liveried servants came in, and announced that the venerable Mother Church requested the favour of a few moments conversation with her. "Show her in John, by all means," was the order given to the servant, " and say, I shall be glad to receive her." But to herself, she said, " What can be the matter now, with my dear old friend, for it is very rarely she comes here to see me."

Mother Church enters, duly preceded by the servant. "My dear old friend," says the old Lady of Threadneedle Street, rising to receive her visitor, "I am glad to see you, pray be seated."

"Thank you," replies the venerable lady, who had just entered, " it is very kind of you to see me. I do not want any pecuniary aid, but, knowing you to be better versed in the ways of the world than myself, I have come to consult you about matters which have troubled me of late."

"Yes," replies the lady of Threadneedle Street, "I have heard of the annoyances you have had, for I still take a deep interest in your welfare, and have learnt that there is much secret plotting going on among a number of disaffected persons, who, envious of your position, want to injure you and cripple your resources."

"I am glad," replied her visitor, "that you know something of what has happened, and the wicked design that these people have in hand, as it will spare me the trouble of reciting to you my present position as regards these matters."

"O yes," replied the Lady of Threadneedle Street, "I generally keep my eyes wide open, and learn much of what concerns my neighbours, as well as what affects myself, though I rarely, like yourself, meddle with matters that do not immediately concern me."

"That is commendable as a general rule," replied her visitor, "but you must know as well as myself, or better, that it is necessary to take active steps to prevent mischief, and to guard against the attacks of cunning and designing men; for, if you knew that there were a number of men fully bent upon getting to some of your treasures to carry them off, and were watching continually for some favourable opportunity to effect their purpose, would you not take all necessary precautions beforehand, and give your servants charge to be on their guard, and prevent, by every possible means, any such design been carried out to plunder you of your property?"

"Certainly," replies the other.

Mother Church continues, "Nor would you listen to the foolish and crafty sentiments that some men would utter, that, if you had some of your treasures taken away, you would be lightened of your burdens, and of some of the anxiety which you must necessarily have in looking after so much; or, that you would then, when lightened of so much, be much freer and be better able to adapt yourself to the requirements of the age,—than in going on, as they would say, in one humdrum, antiquated way. You would at once see that there was a design in these words, and would not for a moment be deluded by them. It would not be mere stuff and nonsense, but something worse; and you would justly suspect the persons of some sinister design in what they said."

"Certainly," replied the Lady in Threadneedle Street. "Nor would I hold any parley or intercourse with such men, but order my servant to shew them out of the door; for it would not require a second thought with me, to see that these men had some nefarious design in hand. Besides, honest men have enough to do in looking after their own affairs; and I have generally found, one of two things happen with men that begin thus to meddle with other people's affairs; either they are neglecting their own affairs, which are perhaps going to ruin, or they mean to purport some wrong; and my servants have special instructions to mark these men and avoid having any dealings with them; no, not even to hold any argument with them, for there is no good in it.

"But what you have just said, reminds me of what happened to me in my earlier days, the account of which has passed out of the remembrance of most men, I suppose. It sets forth the very opposite example to that which you have named, for it shows how an honest man will act, even when the power happens accidentally to fall into his own hands of enriching himself by the goods of another. Shall I relate the story to you?"

"Mother Church : "O, yes! I shall be pleased to hear it."

The Lady in Threadneedle Street continued, "I was one day seated at my desk, engaged in my ordinary duties, when my servant brought in a letter, which had been left at the door. On opening it, I found it to be an anonymous one; but it stated what was enough to alarm one thoroughly; for the writer wished me to know, that he could at any time when he liked, by day or night, enter the strong-room where I kept all my gold and treasures; and bid me look to the security of it. I pondered long over the letter, which was roughly written; and I had the strong-room and the iron doors belonging to it, thoroughly examined, and could not possibly see by what means any one could enter; and at last, I came to the conclusion that it was a hoax, to alarm me unnecessarily; so I began to make light of the matter, especially as nothing transpired, and no attempt was made to rob me. But two or three weeks after this, I got another anonymous letter,—evidently from the same individual,—assuring me, that what he had stated in his previous letter was true, and that he was willing to satisfy me, as to the truth of what he had said. And he went on to state, that if I would be in the strong-room at twelve o'clock at night, on a certain night named, he would come and then shew me how the strong-room could be entered. You may be sure that I began then to regard the matter in a serious light; and was determined to see if the writer would make good his words; so I ordered some of my servants to be ready with lanterns and weapons on the night in question; and a little before twelve at night, we descended to the strong-room; and there we remained awhile as still and silent as death, so that we could hear a pin fall; at last we heard a slight noise, not very far off; then, the clock from the Cathedral, not far distant, boomed out the hour of midnight; as soon as it had ceased, we all listened again attentively and, sure enough, there was the noise again, more clearly heard and nearer at hand than before: we all began to feel uneasy, and to stand on our guard, not knowing what might happen, or how the individual might enter, or what force he might bring with him and perhaps overpower us. Then came the noise immediately under the room where we were; there was evidently some one moving about. Soon we began to see one of the flags moving; then it was gradually raised up, and a man, in working-day clothes, put his head through, and said in some such words as these, 'Now, you find me as good as my word.'

He then related to me how he had been working in one of the sewers, which had needed repairing, that he had come up some distance, and conjecturing that he might not be far from my place, which was of some importance even then, he began looking about; and seeing some flags, he raised one of them up, and found himself where he now was. At first, he told me, he was frightened at the sight of the gold and treasures that were spread around him, and he therefore let down the stone safely in its old place, so that it might appear as if nothing had been disturbed, and determined to let me know of the insecurity of the place. And he subsequently took the steps I have named to make me aware of it. You may rest satisfied that I gladly and amply rewarded the man for his honesty, and took effective means to secure my property for the future.

"But now I would remark, that the men of whom you speak, are secretly working underground, as it were, purposely, to find out a way to get at your property, to carry it off. They have no honest design,—no honesty at heart, like the man I have spoken about,—who felt frightened at touching what did not belong him,—even frightened at the sight and temptation that had come in his way; and could not rest until he had taken means to prevent himself, or any one else, doing wrong.

"There are two things that it appears to me these men, who are troubling you, are wanting in, and they are these,—they want the broad principle of truth, and the broad principle of honesty. They do not scruple to make false statements, and misrepresent matters; and they have this further object in view—to take from you, what belongs to you, just as much as my property belongs to me. I know that I should make a good stand for my own, and use every possible means, not to be unfairly or wrongfully deprived of it. And my dear old friend, allow me to say, that, though you like to live in peace, and to go on quietly, doing your duty in life and attending to your own business,—yet it is nevertheless your business to protect, and even valiantly to stand up for your own, by every lawful means, if needs be, rather than let it be wrested from you by evil men; it is a duty you have to perform,—however unpleasant it may be,—to look well after the substance you possess, for your own well-being, and for your children's sake, and the servants you employ in various parts. It is for their welfare you must think,—for if you have not the means to pay your servants,—they will get other places, for,—do not think me intruding to quote Scripture before you,—we must remember that ' the labourer is worthy of his hire :' and as a general rule,—for men are human,—they will carry their services to the best market, and make the most of the gifts God bestows upon them; here and there you will find some from higher motives serving you faithfully for very little; but as a general rule, I say, you must look for their doing the best they can for themselves in a worldly point of view ; and if you have not the means of giving your servants a proper remuneration for their services, one of two things will happen : you will either have materially to lessen the number of them, or to employ less able men : but either way your children and the people you succour, will suffer. And this, I regard as doubly disastrous. No one has been a better friend to the poor than yourself, in many ways; you have been foremost in promoting the education of their children, and made great sacrifices to effect this ; whilst others buttoned up their pockets, and now want to undo your work ; besides this, you have ever been a friend to the poor and needy in their hour of distress; for though labouring men may keep aloof from you a little, when strong and able to earn wages, yet when sickness and misfortune comes, I know to whom they will first turn; and it will be very sad for them if you should be compelled to leave them uncared for, in any less degree than now. And then again, it will be a great misfortune if you are unable to provide able and well-educated men to instruct the people of the land, or have to depend upon less able and less educated men to do this, who will require less for their services; I must say, I view this state of things to which you may be driven, by the covert efforts of designing men, with some consternation. The poor throughout the land will necessarily, to a great extent, lose their most constant friend, and the rising generation will be less likely to attend to the instructions of men not efficiently fitted for their work. There is already a dislike to religious teaching springing up, and it will, then, increase still more. There will indeed be a decadence in religion; more bigotry and strife; more disaffection and restlessness in the country; and further, if this confiscation of your property takes place, it will, in an effectual manner, put a check, in a large degree, to the dedication of any more property to the purposes of religion and charity; just as it was after confiscation of church property at the Reformation; no one will be disposed to leave anything to the Church, or for the benefit of the poor, if in fifty years time, or even longer, it may be ruthlessly taken away, or diverted from the purpose for which it was left."

Mother Church : " Moreover, if you consider what those in other professions,—in business,—or in the civil service get, I do not think that, as a whole, my servants are extravagantly paid. I allow that there are exceptional cases where the pay seems to exceed the work, and in such cases I am as anxious as any prudent reformers may be to have an alteration made, so that those who have more work may be better paid than some of them are. But regarding the service of the church in the aggregate, I cannot but feel that my servants are underpaid if anything; but what do you say?"

The Lady in Threadneedle Street : " I quite think so too; and I have been of this opinion for some time. And viewing it in the light of a political economist I do not think that the State, or any other body, could bring such an amount of moral and meliorating influences and kindly feeling, as well as kindly action, to bear upon the country throughout, as you do for the like sum of money that you give to your servants. It is a great matter to have an educated gentleman planted in all parts of the country, forming, in numerous instances the only, though a small, centre of enlightenment, civilization, and usefulness;—a person also to whom the poor may resort, as to a friend, in all cases of need. It helps in a material manner to keep the bands of society together, and whilst preventing the poor from lapsing into heathenism, infidelity, and barbarism, this service of yours tends to draw together more the different classes of society, and make them more loyal subjects and better members of society. And, if your services are to be withdrawn, or in anywise decreased or impaired, we shall, I am pretty certain, need a larger increase of prisons and police-officers, or other kinds of persons for the restraint of evil doers; for the tendency of man is to deteriorate, and become evil, when left to himself, without any correcting or elevating associations and influences. And certainly of the two, there is no question that your services should be preferred to that of relieving officers, the police, and the infliction of punishments. Your service is the producing cause of much happiness, good will, and moral strength, throughout the country, which is of the greatest value to the nation. For besides its being needful that you should have educated men in your service, it is not the bare routine of labour they perform which tells, but there is a large amount of love and ardour, of extra labour in the discharge of their necessary duties, and of sympathy with others brought in, which mere money cannot purchase. Leaving, then, the right which you have to your property as a matter of justice out of the question at present, I do not think the State could inaugurate and carry out such a useful and valuable service for the whole nation, and especially for the poorer classes of society, for the sum of money you do. It would, therefore, be a most disastrous event for the country were Parliament to consent to deprive you of your means and substance, which is barely sufficient, as I think also, to carry on your important ministrations."*

* Even the *Times* holds that "if Parliament should ever come to think perfect equality in spiritual things worth any cost, it will probably have to pay a good deal for it, that is, to sacrifice much good service, the place of which it may not be easy to supply. There are no functionaries in the whole world so localised, so hand-tied, so subordinated, and so placed at the mercy of everybody about them as the parochial clergy of England. Even apart from the general scantiness of their incomes and the utter absence of

To which her visitor replied, "I am well pleased to hear you speak as you do, as it shews me that you take a warm interest in what so intimately concerns me, and in the welfare of your neighbours and your poor brethren. But, there is one thing I much fear,—and the thought of it grieves me,—and that is, that the poor or labouring class, whose interest I have so long had at heart, and the evidence of which is not wanting to them,— will be deluded by these plotters and agitators,

what are called prospects, very few Dissenting ministers of education and teaching would submit to the sentence of immobility pronounced on the clergyman who once takes a moderate living. He may have distinguished himself at school and university, and be a scholar, a divine, a man of general information and varied capacity, but there he is generally a fixture for life. The day of his induction he may read over his head that there is no hope for him but in heaven. Fortunate or unfortunate, he will have few minds indeed with which he can hold converse, unless it be on spiritual things. He has to visit the sick and the aged regularly, to cheer the desponding and low-spirited, to superintend and help at the school, to watch, to warn, to chide, and, if possible, to reform. He has to bear patiently with all sorts of follies and absurdities. He has to make up quarrels, and restrain the savageness of untutored minds. There are thousands of such men now in the service of the Church of England—or of the State, as Mr. Miall's friends would put it— in all corners of this land, drowned in fens, hidden in wolds, buried under interminable hedgerows, banished into salt marshes, without the least chance of ever changing their position, should they venture to indulge in so wild a dream. Now, is all this nothing? Is it not worth a notice, a passing allusion, or a slight qualification of the general tone of Nonconformist censure? Truth requires it; and, even where the cause is good and the controversy hot, truth still is the best guide."—*Vide October* 3, 1872.

and induced to turn against me. I trust, however, that the better education, which they have had of late years, will enable them to think for themselves and to see things as they really are, and not to be hood-winked by crafty men, 'who lie in wait to deceive.' These men have thrown out taunting words to depreciate, and even give a wrong colour to, my charitable efforts for the poor, so as to beguile the labouring man, till he almost thinks that my servants are not his friends, and that by helping in the unholy work of despoiling the church he will, somehow or other, have a bank of his own to fly to, in case of need. Now you, dear Madam, know well, that 'the poor will never cease out of the land,' however much their wages be raised; and that opportunities of doing them good, when we will, shall never cease also; for, it must be remembered that the labourers of our land have, in most cases, little opportunity of laying anything by against what is called 'a rainy day;' and have consequently little to fall back upon when misfortune or sickness, some bodily infirmity, or old age, comes upon them; and it is then that they most need a little help, and a kind, comforting word. Besides, our Heavenly Lord and Master has

C

bidden us to care for them, and speak words of comfort to them; and it is hard to have our good misrepresented as evil, and to think that the men who, of all others may find their need of my ministrations, may be led to give their support to those men who are endeavouring to undermine my position."

The Lady in Threadneedle Street took up the conversation, and said, "I must confess I feel for you in this matter, but I trust the labouring class of our land will have the good sense to see, in what direction their own interests ultimately lie: for the great hardship and cruelty of the measure, if ever it is brought about, of despoiling you of your property, will fall, heaviest of all, upon the common people of England, the great body of whom, these plotters and agitators would make use of in gaining their object; in which they themselves, I can see, design to be the greatest gainers, though they don't want the people to think so. The upper and middle classes of society can take care of themselves, if such a confiscation of your property comes about; and even your present servants,—your Bishops and Clergy,—will not suffer any pecuniary loss, for according to Parliamentary usage, their life interest will be secured to them.

It is, I see well enough, the great body of the working people of England and their children after them, who will in the end suffer most, if this spoliation is brought about. The working people of our land have become a great power; and the work of spoliation cannot be done without their aid; and, if ever they become so foolish and blinded, as to give this aid, they will bitterly rue it; for if the time ever comes, when this work of confiscation takes place, the labouring class will see, to their dismay, that they have been injuring themselves most of all, and that they have been led to do this by the misrepresentations, and delusive words of those who have their own ends and purposes to serve. Like the powerful eagle, which was shot by the archer, and is said, in the fable, to have beheld, in the arrow that struck her, its own feathers, which served to guide the deadly weapon to its own breast; or, like the tree which was felled by the woodman, and, in fabled words, is said to have beheld, in the helve of the woodman's axe, which enabled him to effect its downfall, a branch of its own, so will the labouring class of England behold, when too late, that from among themselves have been drawn the very power and aid that has wrought them so much harm and loss."

Her visitor again replied, " I sincerely trust such a disaster may be averted, for it will grieve me to the quick to see the poor suffering and not be able to give them such succour or consolation as I have been wont to do, when they need it; and be obliged to employ an inferior class of men in general to minister in God's service, and to preach in my pulpits. These things I must labour to avert by all possible means, and no efforts of mine shall be wanting to do this. I have already given private instruction to my servants, and the several members of my family in the most important stations where they have been placed, to do all they can to counteract the evil designs of these plotters and agitators; and defence associations have been formed in various parts of the country, with good effect; so you see I have not been idle. But now tell me what you think I may do more to guard against the evil which is threatened: how would you advise me to act?"

The Lady in Threadneedle Street answered: " I was pleased to know, even before you told me, that you were up and on the alert, and I commend you in what you have hitherto done; and I would say to you, 1st, Do not slack your hand in this respect, but carry the work out further, into every part wherever your work lies; rouse up the members of your family in the country parishes, and shew them that, as they will suffer most if a confiscation of your property takes place, they ought therefore to be most earnest in giving you support, and resisting the designs of the enemy. I do not think they are doing their duty in these places, at this crisis; nor preparing for the storm: I know how *difficult it is* to move them in some places, but you must give them no rest; but again, and again, and again, call upon them to do their duty at this time, in every instance where they are backward. Through the agencies you have already established you may be able to effect much of this, so as to carry out your ramifications of defence to all parts."

"This is one thing I should advise you to; and now I have a 2nd matter to mention to you, and that is, that you *strengthen your material position more.* You know that when a city is besieged by an enemy, it is not only desirable to be ready to repulse the enemy on all sides, whereever the assault is made; it is not only desirable to keep those within the city well affected, and in good health, and well supplied with food; but it is essentially necessary, for a more permanent and effective defence,—and that the inhabitants be not taken by surprise in an unguarded moment,— that they should labour to restore the walls that have been broken down, and to repair the breaches. And I cannot but think that your position, my worthy friend, would be materially strengthened, were your people to make an effort to restore your ancient foundations, and again obtain the rights and liberties you once possessed: for, it is just because you are without these, and because they are suffered to remain thrown down, as if they were of no value to you,—that you are so frequently a prey to the inroad of your enemies, so that you can hardly help their depredations, and can only with great difficulty defend yourself."

Mother Church: "Yes, I feel the force of what you say, and I have often wished that I could take the steps that you recommend; but many of my servants are opposed to such a measure, as it might unsettle them; too many love their ease, and feel pledged to keep things as they are; and they fear that, in attempting to obtain a restoration of our rights and liberties, the enemy would make it the occasion of a more direct and open assault upon us. But others of my servants, and very many members of my family, are in favour of such a movement; and I am the more inclined to go with them; for then I should be better able to consult, and adopt measures, with them,—with both clergy and laity in lawful assemblies—concerning the interests of my establishment; and we should thereby be drawn together as one family more, and have a greater and more general interest created in its welfare: for it is absurd to think that this will lead us to greater disunion than there is at present. It is bad enough now. There may be, and especially at first, some contention among my servants for their own several peculiar ways of thinking and acting. I do not see much harm in this so long as they keep within bounds, as there is a diversity of minds, and some latitude of opinion allowed among us; but I do think such a restoration of rights and liberties would vastly contribute to greater unity and devotion and interest among us in the long run, as it would also contribute to our material security, against the inroads of our neighbouring foes.

"But there is this further difficulty that meets me,—that in my present relation or connection with our great and powerful neighbour, Madam

Britannia, I am under restraint in these matters, and I feel under an obligation not to attempt them without leave."

The Lady in Threadneedle Street: "But why not ask leave of Madam Britannia? She would not take it ill of you; and I am disposed to think, that if you set your case fairly before her, you would find her willing to listen favourably to your statements. I know she has an unbounded respect for you, and would be glad to improve your condition, if it were clearly shown to her how she could do this, consistently with the interests of others. She feels too, I believe, that in granting privileges to some of her dependents who differ from you, she has somewhat injured you, and placed you, in more ways than one, in a false and in a more disadvantageous position than you formerly held, and would be the more ready, on this account, to concede your rights and liberties. But between ourselves, the fact is, she requires matters to be urgently pressed upon her; not but that she herself would gladly comply with your desires, at once, when you put the necessity before her; but she has so many different dependents to please, that she hesitates to take any step, however desirable it may be, and often holds back lest she should cause unpleasantness among them, until she finds that her factotum, John Bull, is won over; for she knows that he has such an immense influence, that, whether right or wrong, his opinion is almost law with her. I should therefore advise you to seek an interview with her, and ask as a favour, that her supporter, John Bull, may be permitted to be present at the interview, to hear your statements and requirements;' by this means you will please both one and the other, for they like to work together, with one mind, and you will be more likely to gain what you want."

Mother Church: "I thank you very much for your excellent advice, and shall not fail to act upon it; but I am afraid that I have already trespassed too much upon your valuable time, so I must wish you good morning."

The Lady in Threadneedle Street: "There is one thing, however, I must allude to for one moment before you go, and that is, that you should still be ready to render such special service and co-operation to Madam Britannia as you have hitherto given her, and which she will still need, in carrying on her extensive operations; for both yourself and I are greatly benefitted by her wise rule and exercise of authority. The special service and co-operation I allude to, is that your Bishops, as hitherto, should willingly give the aid of their counsel and advice in Parliament; and that the nation may through the functions of the Church approach God, when it is desirable that her people should offer up, as one man, special prayers, on thanksgiving days, days of humiliation, and other like national occasions. For if the English nation is to retain its character as a Christian nation, it must make a selection of some one body of Christians, as its mouth-piece, through whom it may address the Almighty. This indeed might be done by selecting first one body of Christians and then another; but this would be to introduce another element of confusion and discord, and only defeat the very design of such a change. And since one must be chosen, none has a higher claim than the Church of England, and none other would be so acceptable to the people of England in general, as the Church which from time immemorial has discharged this sacred duty. It is a necessity of the nation, then, to preserve the Church in this office.*

---

* Long will the Thanksgiving Day for the recovery of the Prince of Wales be remembered, for the unity of feeling and national enthusiasm that prevailed among all classes of society ; and it was

And on these grounds, I do not think that Madam Britannia should yield any further to the unceasing demands of those restless, unsatisfied, and never-to-be-satisfied politicians, who would,— to gratify their own whims,—though they call it a matter of conscience,—divest our Constitution altogether of its religious character. She must consider her own welfare and character a little,—and that of the rest of her people. *Disestablishment* has been already carried out far enough, in all necessary ways, so as practically to give all religious rights and liberties to those who dissent from you, Madam.* And it is just because Disestablishment has been thus practically effected in favour of those who differ from you, and landed you in such an equivocal and even hurtful situation,— that I think it the more needful that you should obtain the *Re-establishment* of your own rights and liberties. Pardon me, if I say, that I think

an acceptable fact also to the people at large, that the Church acted as the national mouth-piece in offering up the public thanksgiving to God.

* The present Bishop of Carlisle, in a pastoral letter to his clergy, said, "I cannot shut my eyes to the possibility of a great change coming sooner or later over the *status* of the Church of England : she may possibly cease to be an Established Church—in some important particulars she may perhaps already be said to have done so."

you have been sadly remiss, in times past, from one cause or another, in not looking after them; and I cannot but think, that you might greatly recover them even yet, if you were a little more pressing and persistent in urging your claims."

Mother Church: "You have indeed given me matter for anxious thought, and yet you make me more hopeful for the future; and once more, let me sincerely thank you before I go."

The Lady in Threadneedle Street: "I also feel pleased, dear Madam, with the honour you have done me, in asking my counsel, and listening to me; and, be assured, I shall not fail to take a deep interest in what concerns your welfare."

With this the two ladies rose, and bid adieu to each other. Mother Church pursued her way home cogitating upon the step she was about to take, not forgetting to look upwards for help; and when seated in her own room, she at once wrote to Madam Britannia, asking for an interview, stating her object in a definite manner, and requesting, as a favour, that their neighbour, John Bull, might be permitted to be present. In due course an answer was received, and a time appointed for the interview.

PART II.

ON the day named, and at the appointed time, Mother Church might have been seen winding her way to the mansion where Madam Britannia resided. On her arrival she was met at the door by two liveried servants, and another dressed in black with a wand in his hand, waiting ready to conduct her to the apartment where his mistress was waiting to receive her visitor. Mother Church was one that would, from her very bearing, command respect and attention, and it was now duly paid her; for whilst there was something noble and dignified in her aspect, there was also a calm, yet kind benignity, that beamed from her eyes, speaking of much love and sympathy. Upon being ushered into the audience-chamber, Madam Britannia rose and came forward, and welcomed her guest with due courtesy. John Bull also was present, and rose, making a profound bow: he was dressed, as was usual on great occasions; and Mother Church, after exchanging greetings with Madam Britannia, went forwards to shake hands with him, and to thank him for coming.

John Bull replied, that he himself had on many occasions received much kindness from her, and felt interested in her future welfare; and said, further, that he felt honoured in being called to give her counsel on the present occasion.

Madam Britannia also joined in and said, "Yes, we must all feel indebted to our venerable friend, who has come to consult us about her affairs, for her unvarying kindness and devoted attention to our people; and, indeed, we are so intimately connected with her affairs, that what concerns her, really concerns us, and her welfare is ours also."

Mother Church: "It is kind of you to say this, and the more so, at the present time, when I need your co-operation and support; for as you are aware, I doubt not, there is a thoroughly well organized scheme, or society formed to overthrow the stability of the Church, or do me some material injury, so as to cripple my resources, and compel me largely to reduce my establishment, which of course, will prevent me attending to your people, and affording them that special service and ministry of kindness, that they continually need. What affects me does, therefore, as you say, concern yourself, and any material injury done to me, by the persons I have alluded, will be an injury to yourself also. I have therefore felt the more emboldened to ask your counsel and support in this matter."

Madam Britannia: "Yes, I have heard of this scheme, and have been somewhat troubled at it, for I am afraid it boded no good towards you, my excellent friend; and moreover, it is their design, I hear, to urge me to consent to this measure, for they find themselves unable to effect their object without my leave, and, of course, I am opposed to it, and dislike the idea of such a thing."

Mother Church: "Yes, this is their design, I know. And the way in which they intend to proceed, to compass their purpose, will be this, I believe; to deceive our old friend here, by making him think, that he will be conferring a benefit upon me, by helping them forward in their project; and then having hoodwinked him, they will press upon him from all sides, and give him no peace, till he can persuade you to consent to the measures they propose: for they know, that it will only be at his urgent request, that you yourself, Madam, will feel constrained, however unwillingly, to consent to my undoing: a measure, as it has been said, that will be hurtful to yourself and to our friend here, as well as to myself also. Thus, sir," turning to Mr. Bull, " do they design to make a cats-paw of you, if they can,—an unwitting instrument in furthering my downfall."

John Bull: " Not if I know it, Madam ! But I am glad you have made me aware of this, that I may be on my guard against this vile scheme ; for I must confess, that there are some clever, crafty people that do occasionally get to the blind side of me, and bamboozle me at times, to my great annoyance, when I find it out, afterwards ; for I am thus led to do, what I have sorely to regret having done. I should therefore like to know something more about this business, if you have no objections, lest I should be induced, without knowing it, to do no little wrong and mischief."

Mother Church : " Most gladly will I speak to you further upon the matter, for this was one reason why I wished you to be present, at my interview with Madam Britannia, that you might be made aware of their design, and have your eyes thoroughly opened to what you might expect from them. You know the proverb, ' Forewarned, forearmed,' and I believe it will be so in your case : for if there is anything you are noted for, it is your honest straightforwardness; and your hatred of mere sham and clap-trap; your utter detestation of all kinds of villainy and deception, and none the less, when they come under the garb of friendship or religion."

John Bull: "Well, madam, you are not far from the mark there; I do from my heart abominate these things, and cannot abide them, when I find them out."

Mother Church: "Well now, I want to know, if these people, to whom I allude, have not already intimated—so that it may get to your ears,—their intention to lay before Madam's Parliament a skilfully worded proposal respecting myself,—to the effect, 'that the establishment by law of the Church of England, ought not to be maintained;' (they mention Scotland also, but I will speak only of what concerns myself)—and this, because as they state, 'it involves a violation of religious equality,—deprives me of the right of self-government,—imposes on Parliament duties, which it is not qualified to discharge,—and is hurtful to the religious and political interests of the community.' Now without stopping to consider what they mean by these high-sounding phrases and plausible reasons, just ask these men, if this is all they want,—if there is anything kept back, which does not appear in the face and front of these reasons?. Ask them, if they will consent to deal with the measure on the understanding that the property of the Church is not to be touched?—if there is any design in the Bill which is to be proposed, to deprive the Church of her emoluments and possessions in any way? Thus touch them but lightly with Ithuriel's spear, and see if they do not start up, discovered and surprised! Yes, this is their main object,—to cripple and maim the Church; and yet they keep this back, concealed from you,—hidden behind the mask of specious words, with which they mean to deceive you, my worthy friend, and those you represent,—the great body of honest Englishmen."

"And when discovered, and the mask is torn off, they will soon recover themselves, and tell you of their good intentions towards me,—that I shall be better for the change,—free to begin the world again unfettered."

"And as to the property of the Church, they will tell you,—for they will try to beguile you, in every possible way, and look you in the face all the time,—that they are quite willing, that all the property that really belongs to the Church, should still be retained by the Church, but all that belongs to the nation, should be taken by the nation, and applied to other national purposes."

John Bull: "Yes, this is a point that has much perplexed me; for I was always under the impression that all the property which the Church had, was really hers, and that neither King nor Parliament had a right to it, any further than managing it,—seeing it put to the best advantage for the benefit of the Church, and preventing any waste or abuse. And turning the matter over in my own mind,—for things are said in these days, which puzzle one much, I wondered how it was, that, if any of the property of the Church did belong to the nation, as their own, they did not try to recover it at law, in the usual way people do. They—I mean those who act for the nation in money matters,—are pretty keen in looking after their money, I know; and if any money or property in the Church really belonged to the nation, they would not be long before they were after it; they'd scent it out from far, like a rat;—and this leads me to think that there must be some gammon and befoolery in this way of putting the matter."

Mother Church: "You are right there, Mr.

Bull. The nation has no right to one penny of the Church's money, so as to apply in any other way than for the Church's welfare: and these men, who thus confuse the terms used,—in order to mislead people, talking as if some part, of what the Church now has, belongs properly to the nation, and only part to the Church,—know full well, that the nation has no legal or moral claim to any portion of it, any more than the nation has to that of any of the railway companies, or large hospitals;—and this is the very reason why they want to get an Act of Parliament to enable them to do this; they want Parliament to do a great act of injustice and wrong; and one from which the poor and the labouring man will suffer most; and they might just as well call upon Parliament to pass an act to make other religious bodies, or some of those large hospitals I have alluded to, give up half or a third of their revenues, as they purpose that I should do. The one would be about as just and right as the other."

John Bull: "Well, that has always been my notion about the matter, until these new-fangled terms came into use, which seem to turn things upside down, and to make it appear, as if we knew not what was right or what was wrong; but

I know better than that; and however they may confuse one by talk, there is a right and a wrong in things, which often strikes one at the first, and which I have been led to think, is conscience speaking to a man, which impressions he should stick to, — and especially when he does not thoroughly understand 'the *ins* and the *outs*' of the matter, by reason of the different representations which are made."

Mother Church : "The question of Church property is a long one, when you consider it in all its bearings; but I may just give you a plain and brief view of it, and leave you to think it over further, at your leisure. The Church of England,— which I represent—is called the National Church, because in the early days, when the Church taught Christianity to the people of this land, it came to be acknowledged by the whole nation. As converts were made, and people gradually became Christians, they provided for the maintenance of the clergy and the administration of religion; endowments of land were given, and a portion of the yearly increase was secured to the Church in perpetuity by numerous landlords, that their tenants, and the poor around them, as well as themselves, might have the ministrations of religion secured to them; and when Christianity was pretty generally adopted throughout the country, the ancient Kings and Councils of the realm confirmed and secured to the Church for ever by most solemn oaths, the land and tithes thus obtained. In this sense it may be said to have been *secured* to the Church, *not* '*acquired*, by legislative enactment,' as these agitators state in one of their official papers. And no private person or public corporation can have a better title to their property, than the Church has to her tithes and lands. There are often disputes about the lawful succession to property, but the identity of the Church, as the lawful owner of the property she possesses, is easily and fully to be recognised, generation after generation; as she has in all generations, since it was secured, enjoyed this property, if we except one or two occasions when she was disturbed in her possessions."

"At the Reformation the Crown undertook to be the guardian of this property, and a sorry guardian, I am sorry to say, she proved; for she suffered most of her favourites to help themselves to some of the choicest portions of Church property; for all of what are called 'impropriated lands and tithes,' now in the hands of laymen, formerly belonged strictly to the Church ; however, what remained, was continued to the Church until the Rebellion, when the Church was wholly deprived of this remainder of her property for a few years. It was, however, shortly afterwards restored to her again, and, with various large additions which her children have from time to time given to her since then, it has continued to be hers to the present day, though the Nation is the Guardian or Trustee for it still. Now just consider the question in a clear and simple manner;—if a guardian or trustee appropriated to himself, or to any other person, or to any other purpose than that which his trust implies, the money or property entrusted to him, should we not consider him to be a faithless and dishonest man ? Certainly we should. And if the English nation ever does the like with Church property, she will be none other than unfaithful and dishonest, however these men may gloss over the transaction. England has, hitherto, held a high place among the nations of the earth for equitable dealing and honesty of purpose, but she will then be no longer able to do so.

John Bull : "Thank you very much, Madam.

I understand now better than I did, in what sense the Church of England is a National Church; and still more so what a solid title she possesses to her tithes and lands. I see also that the Nation has no right or business, if strictly honest, to appropriate any portion of Church property to her own ends; and that all the State has to do, is to take care that it be properly applied and to the best advantage."

Mother Church: "Then, as I have said before, these people will want to persuade you that I shall be the better off for being lightened of some part of my property, and will exert myself the more when I am deprived of it;—but this is just what a highwayman or a thief would say when they wanted to get your money: and you must know, with your intercourse with the world, that men of education and ability require to be paid according to what their services would yield; and it is only right that they who devote themselves to religion, in the Church's service, should have an adequate remuneration, as well as those who are engaged in any secular profession or business. Many of these in the Church, as you know, are but poorly paid for what they do; especially considering the high price things have now got to. Why should these agitators, then, want to make the Church less able to support them? They had better try to help her to more;—help her to recover some of those 'impropriations,' which have been taken from her and are now enjoyed by laymen. Besides, there is great need, from the large increase of the labouring population, that I should employ many more well-educated men than I now have, to do the work there is now to be done; so that I want more money than I have to expend, and not less."

Madam Britannia: "I thank you most sincerely, worthy Madam, for putting these matters thus plainly before myself and my able supporter, Mr. Bull; and I also now see, both the justice and the necessity of keeping the property and emoluments of the Church in tact; and not allowing anything to be taken from her, lest by injuring her we injure our people—as I thought we should do by such a measure—and deprive them of those religious advantages which to some extent they now possess, and which they learn to value so highly in their hour of need. I view the matter in a more serious light than ever, and see that it would be inflicting not only an injury, but a grevious wrong, especially upon the labour-

ing class,—for the poor come chiefly from them,
—if your ability is taken away to uphold the
worship of God among them, or to minister to
the people as you now do; for there is no other
religious body that can do what you are now
doing for the people, if you become maimed and
crippled by these confiscations :* and it is a wrong,

---

* An eminent Independent minister, the late Rev. J. Angell
James, in his book entitled "The Earnest Ministry," bears a high
testimony to the valuable services of the Church of England and
her clergy, confirming what has been said, in these words:—
"We must rejoice in their labours and in their success, except
when their object and their aim are to crush Dissenters. There
are very many among them of the true apostolic succession and
doctrine, spirit and devotedness ; many whose piety and zeal we
should do well to emulate : many to be united with whom in the
bonds of private friendship and public co-operation is among the
felicities of my life. Sincerely and cordially attached to the
Church, they are labouring in season and out of season to promote
its interests. Who can blame them ? Instead of this, let us imi-
tate them. Their zeal and devotedness are worthy of it. I know
their labours, and am astonished at them. Think of a Clergyman,
—and multitudes of such there are,—who, besides his other labours,
spends four or five hours every day in going from house to house,
visiting the sick, instructing the ignorant, comforting the distressed.
Can we wonder that such men should take hold on the public mind ?
Is it not the natural course of things that it should be so? It is
admitted that the Clergyman of a parish has advantages for this
species of ministerial occupation which we have not : he considers
all the people within a certain topographical limit as belonging to
him, as being, in fact, his cure: and most of them, if not all of
them, except such of them as by profession belong to other denominations, look upon him in the light of their Minister. This over
active assiduity, in addition to the Lord's-day exercises, is admoni-
tory to us. Can we see this new sight, the whole Church estab-

I fear, that would justly recoil on the nation at large. Already there is a spirit of communism springing up among the people, and gathering strength in the substrata of society; yes, and I have been truly horrified to hear sentiments,

lishment, from the Archbishop of Canterbury down to the curate of the smallest village, with all their comprehensive agency of Pastoral Aid Societies, Ladies' District Visiting Societies, Scripture Readers, Church of England Tract Societies, and other means of influence and power, in big commotion, dotting the land all over with churches and schools, and by all these efforts labouring so entirely to occupy the nation as to leave no room for, and to prove there is no need of, any other body of Christians : can we have all this constantly before our eyes, and not see our need of an earnest ministry, not only if we would maintain our ground, but make any advance?"

Since this was written there has been an astonishing growth of activity and devotedness in the Church throughout the length and breadth of the land, and yet, the political Dissenters of the present day are full of bitter enmity against the Church, calumniating and reviling her in every possible way. How is this strange fact to be accounted for? The Dissenters have had many privileges accorded to them, and it reminds one too forcibly of Haman's words, "Yet all this availeth me nothing so long as I see Mordecai the Jew sitting at the King's gate." Another noted Independent minister, who is no friend to the Church, undesignedly gives testimony to the worth also of her services. The Rev. Thos. Binney, some years ago, in a lecture to Dissenting ministers, at Crosby, said, "My friends, we, as Dissenters, must cease to attempt to multiply little men and little interests up and down the country. All that we must pretend to do is to have well-regulated dissent in our towns, for the purpose of putting the Church of England right. We can do nothing more than that; for the only community in England which possesses the machinery for evangelising the labouring classes, for diffusing the Gospel throughout the length and breadth of the land—the only community is that of the Church of England."

somewhat akin to communism, uttered by one or two in high rank, and by some who are admitted into my service: and, if you are to be compelled to withdraw your services from places where the people are unable to contribute anything like adequate means for the support of your clergymen, I sadly fear we shall have a race of communists springing up in our very midst, who, in a time of change and disquietude, might work incalculable havoc, mischief, and misery, to all classes. We must not therefore suffer any injury to be done to you, in the attempt to satisfy a few restless politicians, whom I am afraid it is in vain ever to think of pleasing; but must faithfully give you what support we can in your wise and zealous endeavours, all through the country, to counteract any such evil as now threatens us. If this evil were to gain the ascendency, it would be worse for us than a German invasion and the horrors of war. These could in time be repaired, but the poison of communism and infidelity would still linger in and corrupt the vital blood and energies of the nation, as it did in France, from the earlier revolutions; requiring it to be kept under with an iron hand, lest it should break out, as it did after the late war.

"But now tell me,—for I want to know your honest opinion about the matter,—do you think that, through my Parliament or the Sovereign, I exercise an authority or control over your actions which I ought not to do, or which is not consistent with my civil position; or that you are thereby hindered in your work: for that is what seems to be implied in the proposition of these restless agitators? And do you think it desirable, and that it would be more conducive to your progress and welfare, as a religious body, that you ought to have more freedom, and should possess in a greater degree than you do at present, the right of self-government of which they speak? I must confess that I have been rather exercised of late in my mind, upon these questions; as my real desire—be satisfied, Madam,—is to do you good and not harm,—to promote your interests, and not to retard your efforts of usefulness by any power which I possess."

Mother Church: "You have put some very delicate, and yet momentous questions before me, but such as I will endeavour openly and truly to answer."

Madam Britannia: "But just allow me to say this much further, first: I am aware that, in order to relieve the consciences of many of my people who differ from you in religious matters, I have felt compelled to make changes which, on several occasions, led me to withdraw from you, or do away with, nearly all those peculiar privileges and advantages which you formerly enjoyed by reason of your connection with the State; and have further, thereby, placed you in an improper and disadvantageous position in the country, as also for carrying on your work. For, as it is well known, Parliament,—which directs my affairs,—was formerly chiefly composed of Church-people; and then your affairs were regulated by a body of Churchmen professedly. Now it is wholly different. Persons of all religions, and of no religion, may be sent to Parliament,—Jews, Romanists, Socinians, and Quakers; Baptists, and Mormonites, as well as Churchmen;—and it must be apparent to all honest minds that this is not the sort of body that should be allowed to canvass matters respecting religion or the Church, and to decide matters for and against you. I feel it to be unfair and unjust dealing towards you; and I think my friend, Mr. Bull, does so too; and I have often seriously wished that some change could be made, so as to place you in a better position, whereby also you might have a more direct control and ordering of your own affairs. I must also say that it would be a great relief to myself, for I have enough to do to mind my own affairs well, without taking the extra burden of managing and settling things for you, which you could and ought to do for yourself, as others do, and would probably do it better and more satisfactorily than I do; for, owing to the difference of religious opinions that prevail, I am often put to much trouble concerning your affairs, and involved in many vexatious disputes, in cases where it is impossible to satisfy all, even when you do all you can, as you think, for the best."

Mother Church: "I see the difficult position you are placed in as well as myself, and I am sorry that you should have so much trouble on my account. It has not, however, been brought on by me, but by those who are opposed to me, and who are projecting means to injure me still further. But referring to the changes which have been made of late years, involving the loss of almost every advantage which I had above others, from my connection with the State, I should almost have doubted whether you were really my friend in what had been done, had I not known how hardly you have been pressed upon to make those alterations alluded to; but I am glad to find that you are still really interested in my welfare. And now to speak of the important subjects you have just named, viz., my freedom and self government. Owing to these changes which have been made, which have materially affected my position and involved both yourself and me in great difficulties at times, I have, after much consideration, come to the opinion,—and it has been growing upon me for years,—that I ought now to be *re-established* in my own rights and liberties,—not in any way to clash with your authority, but in a constitutional manner, for you must ever remain the Guardian of all English rights and liberties;—and that I should be allowed to have the government and control of my own family and affairs more than I have had."

Madam Britannia: "But I thought many of your people were opposed to this, especially your Bishops and leading clergy."

Mother Church: "Yes, this is true to a great extent; but it is not so with all; indeed, in the great body of the Church, there is a growing conviction, that things cannot go on long as they are;

and that it is very desirable, that we ourselves should conduct and carry out the needful changes, and not leave it to those who are agitating the matter, with the design of injuring us. Many dread the change, and well they may, if it is to be left to these men,—lest it be made an occasion of spoliation. But this is just what we must guard against; and our endeavour must be so gradually to guide and direct affairs, as to avoid the rocks and shoals that may be ahead. But there is another reason why many, of those you have alluded to, are opposed to any change as to my possessing self-governing powers,—or are lukewarm in entertaining it, and it is, that they are afraid of offending you; for most of them have been, directly and indirectly, appointed to their present posts through you, and consequently feel bound in some measure to support the system through which they have obtained their position. And this, by the way, is just one of those things which I must speak to you further about, and which I think needs altering; for I do not think it a right thing or conducive to order or peace in my family, that you should have the appointment of my servants, any more than I should have of yours: for generally they think more of your favour and orders than of mine. And though I am usually treated with respect by my servants, yet are there those who will not be guided by me, but set me at defiance; many of those who have been appointed by you think themselves more or less independent of my authority, unless it be strictly ordered by law."

Madam Britannia: "There does seem to be good reason in what you say, but now let me know specifically what changes you would have brought about,—for you have doubtless pondered the matter well over."

Mother Church: "Yes, I have, Madam, and with much thought and prayer. But to be brief, I would endeavour to bring about these changes: of course, they will need considering more fully.

I. That the Church should in future have the election of her Bishops and other chief clergy in her own hands. Other religious societies and companies of men, have the appointment of their directors, and chief officers, and it ought to be so in my case. It was so in the primitive days of Christianity, and a long struggle was made to retain it, but it was wrested out of the hands of the Church at last.

II. That the Church should be allowed to

extend her system so as to meet the requirements of the times and the growth of the population. I would have almost every Archdeaconry made into a Bishopric: some might even be too large for a Bishopric, and others too small, so that in some instances alterations would be needed; and this done, we should not then come up to the standard projected at the Reformation; for there would still be twice and a half as many again in population, in each of these re-formed Dioceses, as there would have been then, if the hopes of our Reformers had been carried out.

III. That the Lay-members of the Church, should have a share in the government of the Body, instead of Parliament. And that they should take a part in the election of Bishops for their respective Dioceses, voting by representation with the clergy; and be consulted on all measures of moment respecting her interests, so that nothing be passed without their sanction.

IV. That the autonomy of every Diocese be re-established; that the clergy and laity with the Bishop at their head should assemble in Synod for a few days every year, and proceed to business; that each Diocese be self-governing; but subject to the decisions of a higher assembly.

V. That while the Provinces of Canterbury and York still retain their respective jurisdictions, the whole Church of England should assemble in National Synod once a year; and proceed to business: the whole of the Bishops forming the upper house, and two or four, or more, as it may be deemed desirable, of the representatives of the clergy and of the laity from each Diocese, form the lower house, and vote by order, when they desire to do so.

VI. That the Church in Synod, should have 'power to decree Rites and Ceremonies,' and exercise 'authority in controversies of Faith;' and that in cases of dispute their decision shall be final, without any appeal to a civil tribunal, unless the case, in some way, comes under a breach of the civil law.

VII. That some moderate, yet effective and speedy method of Discipline be re-established in every Diocese, whereby disorders may be corrected, and sound teaching may be maintained. A small judicial body might, by consent of all,—Bishops, clergy and laity,—be appointed to determine cases in each diocese, subject to an appeal to a similar body, elected by the National Synod, to determine and dispose of all cases finally, except as before named, when they come under a breach of the civil laws.

VIII. That the Right of property belonging to the Church, should be more distinctly recognised as such, to be used for the work of the Church, and not applicable to other purposes: the Church to have a more active concern in the disposal of it, or the rearranging of its disposal: not that you should entirely give up your control, but that your officers be guided by my people in Synod, or by a committee appointed by them, respecting its application; your control extending only to a veto upon any disadvantageous or improper use of it. Your officers to be paid out of the property as hitherto."

"Now this is a rough and naked outline of those changes which I would respectfully submit to you for your consideration, respecting *the re-establishment* of my rights and liberties. There is much that I would say on each of these several points, but I must not now trouble you, as I have already trespassed too long upon your time."

Madam Britannia; "Do not say so; I am more than ever interested about the subject, and my time could not have been better occupied. I have learnt much to engage my mind for some time to come, and I shall give the subject a thoughtful and careful consideration; I shall also hope to have the pleasure of conferring with you again about the matter, as I should like to be better informed upon the points you have named, before I make up my mind, as to what I shall do."

John Bull (turning to Mother Church) : " I have listened to you with wrapt attention, for there are some things you have named that quite excite my curiosity and interest, and I hope I shall be allowed to be present at any future interview, upon the subjects that have just been proposed, as I really want to know more about them myself, too. Besides I think them of vast importance to the whole community."

Madam Britannia (addressing herself to Mother Church) : " There may be some points in which I shall agree with you, and some probably in which I may not; but does it not appear to you that by these measures the supremacy of the Sovereign will to some degree be overthrown or damaged?"

Mother Church: "Not if rightly and constitutionally considered, I think. Hitherto we have been too much guided in our views of this matter by Court sycophants of past days,—both among lawyers and divines, as well as statesmen, who, to bask in royal favour, have prompted the Sovereign to use her power to suppress in many ways the rights and liberties of the Church, or to exercise them instead of the Church. Now rightly viewed, I contend that the supremacy of the Crown is designed and held for the purpose of maintaining and upholding the rights and liberties of the people, not of suppressing them—be it in causes ecclesiastical or civil,—or be it towards the individual subject or any society of subjects: and that the utmost amount of freedom in all cases should be afforded, consistent with the general good of the community, and the safety of the temporal government. The safety of the Crown, I also contend, must be upheld in its integrity, and the constitutional exercise of it also, as it is essentially necessary to good government that a supreme power be placed in some hands, not only for the sake of the Church, but for the order and well-being of other societies and orders of men; and then this supremacy, when thus rightly exercised, is one of the brightest jewels that rests upon a Sovereign's brow, which is only dimmed and disfigured when used despotically, to tread upon the rights and liberties of any of the people."

Madam Britannia: "You put the matter in a strong light, still there is much that commends itself to our approbation. But there is another point I want to ask you about, for I must canvass both sides of the question with you, Will not this *re-establishment* of the Church in her rights and liberties, so as to give her a self-government, be the setting up of an *Imperium in Imperio*,—the erecting a kingdom within a kingdom,—the establishing a power which may defy any temporal authority; for thus, it has been intimated to me, that it will be? Would there not be some danger of weakening my civil government by such a measure?"

Mother Church : "Oh, no! this is a foolish notion which some minds are apt to conjure up, as if there were a lion in the way, which will prevent any kind of advancement. If I were under the Pope, or laid claim to exercise authority in civil matters, there might be some apprehension of this danger; but as the Church of England I do not make any such pretensions, for the Church is a kingdom in another sense to that over which a temporal sovereign rules : the one is a spiritual, the other an earthly kingdom, and you need be under no fear of your authority being defied or damaged from the re-establishment of those rights and liberties, whereby

I shall obtain self-government, any more than you are from other religious bodies, and from other large and powerful companies of men. Besides, I trust and honestly think that you would have no more loyal supporters in your dominions than my people, or more amenable to your laws. The supremacy of the Crown would still be maintained, over all causes ecclesiastical and civil: you would have, as you now have, a civil power over all denominations of religion, as well as over men in secular capacities; not indeed to trample upon their rights and liberties, but to prevent wrong, and to uphold the rights and liberties of all alike; and if one or other transgressed the civil laws, they would still be subject to the decisions of your courts of justice."

Madam Britannia: "I thank you for satisfying me on this head, for I can see my way clearer to consenting to such a change as you suggest. But how will you be able to make provision for the creation of so many more dioceses as you think would be desirable? for of course you must not expect any pecuniary assistance from me, as I have other subjects who are dissenters, and they would not regard it as fair, so I am barred from helping you in this way."

Mother Church: "We do not look for help from you in this way; but I think, by a little rearrangement of our resources, which I point to under the eighth head of Rights,—a moderate, though perhaps not quite an adequate income, might be obtained at first, which might be supplemented afterwards by the devotions of the people, which I have no doubt would be forthcoming, especially if it become apparent that the Church's right to her own property would be maintained, as that of other bodies is, and that the sentiments of those who would be levellers and equalizers of the Church's funds were not to prevail."

"It is too large a question to enter upon now; but, in passing, I might suggest as one way of meeting the difficulty, that since the present dioceses would be materially diminished the Bishops should severally hold the office of Dean also in their separate Cathedrals; each Bishop having two Canons under him, constantly resident and ready to supply his place when absent, so that he might feel fully at liberty to go about his diocese as hitherto. Some of the Bishops also might feel disposed to part with a portion of their income, having less responsibilty, and in consequence of their having less demands upon their charity. But however this might be, it might be ordered that upon the appointment of every fresh Bishop a portion of the income,—say a thousand pounds,—should be secured for every new diocese. This,—with the incomes of the Deans and of the Archdeacons, (the office of which, as at present, should be done away with,)—might be one way, among others, of obtaining means for carrying out the extension of the system on the large scale which I have proposed. Of course, this could only be done gradually, and after having been well considered and matured in all its details by your officers, in conjunction with my people in their Synods. I trust, however, that on the increase of Bishoprics you would not require any more Bishops in Parliament than now sit there; for the sacrifice of their time to their parliamentary duties is a serious loss to the several dioceses, where their time and presence is more than ever needed: still we must not begrudge the cost of the services of those you now have when you are consulting for the welfare of the nation, in which we ourselves are also included. Nevertheless, I trust that the services of those you now have will be sufficient, and that there will be no necessity to call for more Bishops to enter Parliament."

Madam Britannia: "You may set your mind at rest upon this point; as I do not think there will be any necessity for more Bishops in Parliament; nor do I think it would be approved of by the nation. Those additional Bishops would then be of more than ordinary service to you."

Mother Church: "Yes, they certainly would; they would be eminently serviceable. I would also remark, before we close our interview, that in what I have proposed for the *re-establishment* of our rights and liberties, in order that we may obtain self-government, there is, I consider, no unreasonable demand made. I have asked for nothing,—for no extra privilege or advantage,—but what other religious bodies in the country already possess, or may possess if they will. You are not asked to concede anything to me, but what you have already conceded to them; and I regard it as only a matter of even-handed justice, which must approve itself to honest-hearted men, and I think to our friend here, Mr. Bull, that since I have suffered loss in other ways, I should at least be made equal to them in the rights and liberties which they already possess."

John Bull: "Well, there is a good deal of truth and reason in what you say, Madam. I do like to see fair play and justice done all round to every one. I was a little startled at first, at some things you said, but I begin to think that it is the right way to meet these difficulties, and to put things upon a better footing throughout the nation. There is nothing like taking the bull by the horns, as the common saying is,— excuse my punning on my own name. And I verily believe that the bringing forwards of a large and bold measure, like what you, our venerable friend, have proposed, and which seems to go to the root of the matter, will put a stop, more than anything else, to these endless bickerings and disputes about religious privileges; and more effectually secure the Church in her posessions, than any thing you could otherwise do. The tinkering measures, as to whether you cannot find something more for the Deans and Canons to do; and the endeavours to obtain only two or three more Bishops, may well stick fast, for they do not meet the requirements of the times in any adequate or proportionate degree."

Here Mother Church rose and said she hoped they would excuse the length of time she had trespassed upon their attention; and thanking them warmly for their consideration of these matters that more especially concerned herself, she took her departure.

John Bull, however, accompanied her to the door, and detained her a moment in the hall, to bid her be of good heart, as he should stand by her and see fair play done. "I'll take care," he said, "to let all those whom I represent know the full truth about all these matters, so that they may have their eyes opened a little, and not be taken in by the gross misrepresentations about you, which are now going about the country. But let me beg of you also, dear Madam, not to relax your own efforts, not only to bring about the *re-establishment* of your rights and liberties, but to keep your people in every part, well informed about matters, and ready to act, as one man, from every point, anytime, at a moment's notice."

Mother Church: "Thank you, my friend, I will not forget what you say, and now, may God's blessing rest upon you." "Amen," replied John with great warmth and reverence; and so they parted.

PART III.

ABOUT three weeks after the last conference with Madam Britannia, Mother Church received a note from her, and upon opening it read as follows: " Madam Britannia presents her compliments to Mother Church, and would feel highly gratified to have the favour of another interview with her on Monday next, at Eleven o'clock, and she further begs to acquaint Mother Church, that should it be convenient for her to come at the time named, she will take care to inform their friend, John Bull, that he may be present."

A satisfactory answer was returned in the affirmative, accepting the invitation; and, at the same time, Mother Church begged permission that she might also bring her friend with her, viz., the Old Lady living in Threadneedle Street. On the day and at the time appointed then, Mother Church, accompanied by her friend, found herself seated in conclave with Madam Britannia and John Bull.

After the usual greetings and interchange of courtesy,—for an old fashioned courtesy as well as cordiality was maintained,—Madam Britannia opened the conference by saying, that she had given much thought and consideration to the matters that had occupied their attention at their last interview, as she felt them to be of great moment, and such as greatly affected the welfare of her people. "And" she continued "you must know that our last interview has already been noised abroad; and, as it is generally known that I am now entertaining considerations respecting an equitable adjustment of those disputed matters, arising from your connection with the State, which seem to cause offence to some, those who are opposed to you, most venerable Lady, urge upon me still the necessity of disconnecting you wholly from the State,—pleading that they also are subjects of the realm, and ought to be placed upon a footing with you, or rather that you should be placed upon an equal footing with them. They assure me also, that my Parliament has full power and authority to dispose of your property as they like, that it is national property; and that as a matter of equity between yourself and them, you should be disposessed of it, or to such an extent as to place you on a level with them."

"Now, I must have you, and all with whom I

am concerned, fully to understand, that it is my wish, and it shall be my endeavour also, to do justly and equitably to all parties, and that each and every one in these dominions should be fairly dealt with, so that there may be no *reasonable* ground of complaint. But whilst I say this, I am conscious, at the same time, that there are some people who have only a one-sided view of fairness,—*i. e.*, fairness towards themselves, and do not consider others ; and will permit injustice and wrong to be done to others, and even approve of it, and regard it in the light of a virtuous act, so long as it brings some advantage to themselves ; and on the other hand, they will continue to complain even when a righteous decision is made, and equitable measures are dealt out to others as well as themselves, if the measures or decisions do not give them some advantage over their neighbours, or come up to their own view of what *they think* ought to be their due : and they are displeased, dissatisfied, and cry out for further justice, if their unjust demands are not yielded to, however hard, or inconsiderate the yielding to their demands might bear upon others. I cannot then for one moment sanction or support such a one-sided kind of justice or equity,—which is no justice or equity at all : I cannot hold the balances in my hand, and give a pressure to the scales on their side, to the injury and detriment of others : nor is there any end, I am apt to think, to such demands and views, when once admitted; for it is but the admission of selfishness—a base craving for what is not theirs, as well as a perversion of justice."

"And I say this, because from what you said on a former occasion,—and I think you have a perfect right to be heard, as well as others,—I was led to think you had the right on your side; for I considered that the measures which have been passed in former years, giving religious liberty and advantages to Dissenters which they did not formerly possess, ought not to place you in more disadvantageous circumstances, with regard to the management and administration of your own concerns, than those which they possess themselves; and that it is only reasonable that you should have your just rights and liberties restored to you, to make you now equal with them; and that your Right to property, however much larger it may be than what they possess,—for you have had a much longer service than they—should be respected as much as theirs; and that nothing—not a hoof or nail—should be taken from you, as belonging to the nation, unless the nation can prove that it has a clear right and substantial title to it, independently of yourself. This, I think, will approve itself to all honest men, and I am sure it will to my friend, Mr. Bull, as even-handed justice."

John Bull: "Aye, aye, Madam! this is the right sort of justice! I like none of those levelling and communistic notions, which seem to me like the principles of the light-fingered gentlemen, who want to be handling, and getting hold of other folks property, rather than earning an honest livelihood for themselves, and living in peace and good-will with their neighbours."

Madame Britannia: "I am glad to hear you speak out, Mr. Bull, as it helps to confirm me in the view I have taken of the matter; and I was only going to add, that as the mist, with which the subject has been enveloped, clears away, so that we can get to see the matter properly in all its bearings, I begin to view the design of confiscating the property of the Church with greater abhorence than I did. It is not only a dangerous movement, which, whatever people may say, will seriously shake the rightful possession of all other kinds of property, and leave things in a very unsafe condition;—it is not only a scheme fraught with harm to the wellbeing of the Church, if not to the very maintenance of true religion, and consequently to the real welfare of the people;—but it is an unjust thing to do, on the very face of it; and no good will come of it to the nation, I am persuaded."

Mother Church: "I truly thank you Madam for your earnest and faithful consideration of the matter I brought before you on a former occasion, and I am glad to learn that you have formed so favourable an impression of the justice of my cause, and that I shall not have appealed to you in vain for protection and support in the obtaining and maintaining my true rights and liberties: especially in such ways, as they have been granted to others, and are truly in accordance with the fundamental constitutions of the realm, and the principles of good government. And let me say this dear Madam, before I begin to speak upon the subject before us, that I firmly believe, it is your earnest wish and determination to do only what is right and just in the matter; and that after ascertaining what is really due to all parties, you will endeavour to give a righteous judgment. It has been the thought of this, that has emboldened me to bring the matter before your notice, because I felt assured, notwithstanding the outcry that is made against me, and the assault which is projected, —and I am sure I have given no real occasion for one or the other,—that wherever Britannia rules there the true principles of liberty and justice will prevail, and predominate."

" I am sorry to have to say it of those who are my neighbours, and with whom I would live in peace, that however plausible their manners, and whatever sentiments of wishing me well they may utter, they are acting as my bitter enemies; I have been very unwillingly forced to this conclusion, especially with regard to some of whom I thought better; but let this pass; let us come to the points in dispute. I have to complain that they grossly misrepresent the true state of the case, as I hope presently to shew you ; and there is, further, so much sophistry mixed up with their statements, that unless you thoroughly examine the subject for yourself, without taking it at second-hand, or on what they say about it, you, and others who wish to do what is right, would be deceived, and think they had some real grievance against me, and that justice demanded that I should be thrown overboard, and my prospects and property should be sacrificed for them. Let me however give you some instances, which will lead us to the very marrow of the question."

"You have just alluded to my having *a Right to property*, as well as other parties; the which, as you may remember, is one of those Rights which ought now, I contend, to be more fully acknowledged by the State, so as to set the matter at rest. Now it is advanced by our adversaries that the Church has no right to property because she is a National Church. But, I would ask you, and all the people of England, or such of them as will but think a moment for themselves, and judge what is right:—why ought not the Church to have a right to property as well as any other religious body in the country? Why should the fact of her being a National Church be any objection to this? Is not this the very reason, think you, why the State *should* acknowledge and firmly maintain the right which the Church has to property, and this, just because her services are administered for the benefit of the whole nation, and not for a sect? If people choose not to have the services of the Church, they are at liberty to have others, and make as many sects in the country as they like, and as many priests and ministers of their own as they will; there is now no law of the land to prevent them. But they have no right to take away the means which the Church possesses for still carrying on her advantageous work,—advantageous as it undoubtedly is to the country. A young man who wants to set up in business, may leave the old established firm, where he has been employed, and begin for himself, but he has no right to take away any of the property belonging to the old firm; or take means to upset its credit or stability, so that he may flourish the more, if he could, by any means, damage it, or cripple its operations. Honest competition and fair dealing he has a right to, and may succeed by them in gaining a footing,—but he has no right to any underhand schemes for ruining the old firm from which he has separated himself. If the Church were supported by the State,—if the country were taxed to maintain the clergy and the services of the Church, or if the State had any just or legitimate claim to the property of the Church,—then, I grant you, our adversaries and opponents might have some just cause to complain, that they were not fairly dealt with. But, as this is not the case even in the smallest degree, as I shall be able to shew you:—and, as I shall be able, on the other hand, to prove that the Church maintains herself on her own property, and on the voluntary contributions of her people;—that she does not get one penny from Parliament, and is no more supported out of the National purse than the Dissenters are, then, I deny that they have any just cause for complaint."

John Bull : " Yes, I see. You have just hit the point there, Madam: and I am anxious to learn further about the matter."

Mother Church : " Then again, take another instance of their sophistry with which they would blind the eyes of the people. They tell you, as it appears, 'that your Parliament has the power and authority to take away, and dispose of the property of the Church as they think fit.' It is true, I grant you, that they have *the power and authority* to do this; but I deny that they have the *right* to do this. They have no right to take what does not belong to them, and appropriate it to their own use, any more than I, or another person has to take what does not belong to us. This, in plain language, is to steal, and those who do such things we call thieves. And it is none the less criminal and immoral for those intrusted with the supreme power and authority in the land to do this. It is an abuse of power,—it is tyranny—the subversion of right to might—the recourse to the principle of the brute force of a barbaric age ; and is equally to be reprobated in the government or legislation of a country, as in the conduct of an individual."

" Parliament has the *power* to confiscate other kinds of property in this country. It can seize upon houses as well as lands, and upon the furniture in the houses, and the wine in the winecellars also. It might seize upon the money in our banks, or pass a law to remit the national debt—wipe it out as discharged, as they did on one occasion the debts of Henry the VIII. ; or they might make a law that no man should possess above a certain moderate amount of money, or land, and that all above that amount should go into the national purse ; or, that when a man dies, half his money or landed property should go to the State. All such things they have power to do. And in discussing the making of such a law, to effect any such scheme, many very plausible excuses and specious arguments might be advanced for passing such a measure. It might be urged, that no man wants more than a competency for himself and his family ; and, that so long as this is secured to him he has enough, and that a more satisfactory use might be made of the surplus, by applying it to the benefit of the nation at large. Or it might be said, that money and property would do more good by being spread among a larger number, than in being confined to a few favoured individuals. You might find some of the advocates for such a law quoting from the poets, and saying:

> 'Man wants but little here below,
> Nor wants that little long.'

Or it might be said, that in all legislative measures we should have the good of the many in view rather than the few. I mention such pleas that you may see how easy it is, for the advocates of such measures, to blind the eyes of those whom they want to cajole and delude; and that many specious arguments might be employed as a pretext to seize upon other kinds of property as well as Church property, *if you once set aside the fundamental principles of right and justice,* or once take away the barrier against fraud, wrong, and robbery; or cease to maintain that you have no right to take from another, without his free will and consent, anything that truly belongs to him,—whether it comes to him by his own exertions, or by inheritance, or by a free gift."

"I will not now enter upon the evil of such a course, and how detrimental it would eventually prove to the whole nation, as it would tend to repress the very springs of industry and laudable ambition ; and how it might be brought to bear also, by legislation, upon the honest industry of the poor, and the skill of the able workman; but I am sure, that amid all the sophistry with which such schemes of confiscation might be advanced there is—as it must strike you all—a false ring about them, which should make you doubtful of accepting them, and set you upon your guard against giving them currency. For the doctrine or principle,—whether it applies to the property of the Church, or of any other corporation, or of an individual,—of taking away from them what is theirs by right, is to be denounced as barbarous and unjust to the extreme. It is but reverting to the principle of savage and lawless times—when they said :—

> 'There is a simple plan,
> That they shall take who have the power,
> And they shall keep who can.'

We therefore protest with all our strength against such schemes, as most pernicious and villainous, as well as most unjust, cruel, and uncalled for."

The Old Lady from Threadneedle Street here exclaimed. "And a most disastrous state of affairs we should have in the country ! No kind of property would be safe; much uneasiness, and a feeling of insecurity would prevail, which would prove very detrimental to the enterprise and interests of the country. There are some of our Statesmen that would pooh-pooh such an opinion, but they do not know as much as I do about these things, or consider what the ultimate results would be. I therefore, as the representative of other kinds of property, not belonging to the Church, would denounce the principles of confiscation as dishonest and unrighteous; for there is no justice in it—unless the party or parties have done some wrong, or abused their right as honest citizens, and then it is a matter for the law to decide upon."

Mother Church : "If Parliament were to act in this way, it would certainly tend to undermine the foundations of our social life in England; and destroy in some measure that sense of right and justice, which exercises so valuable an influence in all the transactions of the Commercial life, and among the trading portions of the community. And as the evil that men do often comes back upon themselves, so is it with the measures of Parliament also; there are many instances in which the country has suffered from the arbitrary and unjust laws which past Parliaments have passed : and Parliament ought now still to fear—however utilitarian and philosophical it may become—that a just retribution would come back upon them if they sanctioned the confiscation of Church property. Parliament, or the State, or the Government are not the *owners* of Church property, but *the trustees* or *guardians* of it, as it has been said over and over again. They never gave this property to the Church, and for the simple reason that they never had it to give; it belonged to the Church, when they came into power, trace successive Parliaments or Governments back as far as you can. Whatever kind of Government or rule came into office or power, they found the Church had property of her own, which belonged to her, and which it was the duty of any Government having the supreme power, to guard and protect. We assert then, without the slightest fear of contradiction, that the supreme power in a realm—whether lodged in the Sovereign, Parliament, or the Government of the day,—is a most responsible charge intrusted to them, to do what is right and just to all, and to uphold and maintain the rights and privileges of all to their utmost extent; and, not to commit a wrong arbitrarily upon any party or section of the community, or to perpetrate gross acts of injustice upon a large scale.

For if they do this, they not only basely abuse the power or authority, which they have in trust, but they frustrate and misconceive the very end or object for which they exist, or have this power and authority given to them. I trust Madam, you will not be offended at my speaking out to you in all plainness and fidelity, and perhaps a little warmly, but you must excuse me; for the subject is one which affects me much, as indeed it does yourself also."

Madame Britannia: "Oh no, I am far from being offended, though the subject fills me with much concern. I quite agree with the general principle you have just enunciated, and I would rather learn the truth, and know how I ought to act rightly and justly in all matters that concern the interest of these realms."

Mother Church: "There is a point further that I would fain bring before you. Why is it that these political dissenters are now clamouring for the confiscation of Church property? Why is it that they purpose, by a side measure, to get Parliament to pass a law to effect this? Is it not from their jealous envying of the goodly heritage I possess? Is it not from the promptings of this base passion, which lie at the bottom of their nefarious designs, and is the main-spring of their zeal and unceasing efforts? Of course they will not allow this for a moment, and will charge us with being uncharitable. But it is nevertheless true. Just apply the measure to themselves, and see how they would take it. Put them for a moment in our position,—regard them as possessing from time immemorial the property that my people do; and we were to want to take it from them, would they not regard it as a villainous and shameful attempt to deprive them of their lawful property; and speak of it as a most intolerant scheme—a system of persecution. And so indeed it would be; and yet they cannot see that they are doing this very thing, and acting in the very way which they would be sure to reprobate in others. But are they not hereby setting aside one of the very fundamental precepts of Christianity by such proceedings; and forgetting the royal law of Christ our Lord—to do to others, as they would that others should do to them? There is only one small ground of excuse for them, however, which we should in justice name; they have been accustomed to cry out for toleration, and have learnt with their mother's milk to have a grievance against the Church, that they would not be happy, and could hardly exist, unless they could find out something to make a noise about, and about which to agitate the country; even now, though they have gained full religious liberty. Many of their preachers also, find that their system of religion thrives the better by keeping up a little round of abuse against the Church; they even advocate it, and are glad to get hold of any tale of scandal, to retail it out. This is however but to foster the seeds of envy, jealousy, and discontent at another's superiority; and having been taught this from their youth up, we must expect outbreaks and attacks at times, and on a larger scale from the most enthusiastic among them, who will not let the rest live in peace. It is nevertheless wrong and mischievous."

John Bull: "This is a notion which has dawned much upon my mind of late years, when I notice one assault after another that has been made upon the Church. These political dissenters have got every civil and religious liberty, I conceive, that they need, for the fair and honest maintenance of their Societies. I should just like them to name one that they haven't; they would find it difficult to do so. And it strikes me that it would look much better of them, if they were to let other folks alone more, and not be for ever meddling with other people's affairs, and causing such constant disturbance in the country. It would be more Christian-like, to my thinking, if they were to mind their own affairs more, and attend to their religious duties more, trying to live in peace with all men, and endeavouring by all the means they can to promote the gospel of our Lord and Saviour; there would not be so much room or time then, for this bitter persecution against the Church, nor for urging intolerant measures and cruel usage towards those whom they should regard, at least, as fellow Christians."

Madam Britannia, addressing Mother Church: "I have said that I freely admit the general principle you have enunciated, and purpose to do my best to uphold it. I must also candidly confess that I think these political dissenters have hitherto failed to make good their statements and assertions. I have seen a number of them in the papers, and then very shortly they have been met and contradicted upon good evidence, so that they appear as calumnies, wantonly uttered, to make the minds of the people evil affected towards the Church: and calumny, when openly exposed, rebounds upon the utterer, and damages the cause he is wishful to further. They have failed, it appears to me, to shew that the tithes, or other endowments of the Church were originally *given*, (though they were certainly confirmed,) by Act of Parliament, or, that Parliament is at the present time granting anything out of the National fund or taxes of the country towards the support of the Church. And therefore, I feel in justice bound to acknowledge that the Church has a right to her property, and must be maintained in her possessions, until it can be clearly proved that the nation has a prior claim or right to the property, independently of the Church. For this is the course that would be taken in a court of justice: no man can be disturbed in the enjoyment of his property, until some one else can give undoubted evidence that he has a prior and superior claim over the property to the individual who is in possession of it. Nor is the individual in possession bound to produce his title-deeds until some such a claim has been established, and then only for the purpose of shewing that he has a more valid right to the property than the person wishing to establish a right. And this, venerable Lady, I take to be your position at the present time, and so far, as I can see, no one has a right to disturb you in your possessions, not even Parliament or the Nation, until they, as a Parliament or a Nation, can substantiate a better claim to the property than you have, and which, you assert, they cannot; for I now fully understand the difference between the Parliament or the Nation having the power to do a thing, and their having a right to do it; and moreover I trust that the Parliament or Nation will never be so weak as to yield to this base jealousy of spirit, or be so worked upon, as to exercise their power in any other way than to maintain what is right and just."

"But now," continued Madam Britannia "might I ask, whether you have anything to show as title-deeds for your property and endowments; or can you give any satisfactory proof of the origin of tithes, as to how the Church, in the first instance, came into possession of them, so as to possess a right to them legally,—and, 'that your endowments cannot be regarded in the light of a grant as continued by the Parliament or Nation for the support of religion : and that your Right should therefore be maintained by them ; taking it for granted that the Parliament or Nation wish only to do what is morally lawful and right ?"

Mother Church : " Most gladly will I furnish you with such proofs and documents as I possess to show you my indisputable title and claim to the property I possess ; and I am the more pleased to do this, and that you have furnished me with the opportunity, because it will serve to put to silence many of those vague and calumnious insinuations about my possessing the property I do,—those random insinuations and misrepresentations, which they fling about to damage my cause in the minds of the people."

John Bull : " I should be right glad if you would do this, worthy lady; for to tell you the truth, I have been sorely puzzled of late, by some of the statements which your adversaries have put forth. I felt in my own mind that you were in the right, and they were the aggressors, but still when you read such words as they put forth, it confuses one ; and one would like to have them not merely contradicted, but proved to be false."

John Bull, during the latter portion of his words had been pulling out of his pocket two or three papers, small books and pamphlets, and began to read portions. "One Edward Miall, says of Parochial tithes, they 'are the product of the public law exclusively, ecclesiastical or civil, or both, and that they neither did, nor in the nature of things, could originate in private liberality."* 'Indivi-

---

* Miall's 'Title-Deeds of the Church of England,' p. 5, Ed. 1871. Miall is chiefly indebted to Selden for his facts, which he colours and twists to suit his purpose, as it has been amply shewn by Pulman. Miall arrives at an opposite conclusion to Selden ; for Selden would not have Tithes to be taken from the Church ; but Miall would, and labours to show why. So true is it, that where one will suck honey another will extract poison.

dual spontaniety never had room to play in the creation of liability to tithe. That liability was from the beginning of the system fixed upon every subject of the realm, not by his own election, in obedience to pious impulses, but by the will of those who had rule over him in Church and State.'† Again he says 'the fact that we have on record such a continuous succession of laws for the payment of parochial tithes, for the period of about four hundred years of the earlier history of the country, is utterly inexplicable on the hypothesis of the tithe endowment system having had its origin in the spontaneous liberality of individuals.'‡ Another, who acknowledges to his being inspired by 'Miall's Title-Deeds of the Church of England,' which he condenses, says, 'we affirm that these endowments are the property of the nation, and absolutely at the disposal of the National will.' Again, 'but further, Parliament might change the constitution of the Established Church. Its discipline, doctrine, and ceremonies lie completely within its control. It has the power to grant all that the Ritualists desire. It might narrow down the system to the meanest conception of the meanest Evangelical. No one can deny that

† Ibid, page 5.   ‡ Ibid, page 26.

its power in this direction is unlimited.' Again! 'The chief endowment of the Church is that of tithes. Our opponents assert that tithes originated in gift and bequest: that in some far distant age land owners voluntarily bestowed upon the Church a tenth of the produce of their land, and that they did this for themselves, and for those that should come after them for ever. This is a broad assertion, lacking only in proofs. No deed is extant, no deeds are known ever to have existed. The claim of a Rector or Vicar is never granted upon deed. He claims his tithe of common right. His tithe is not by virtue of any deed existing, or supposed to be existent, or supposed some time or other to have existed. His claim is a claim of common law. How the tithe system came into existence cannot be affirmed with certainty. But it can be affirmed with certainty that our Clergy have no claim for tithe except that which they derive from the law of the land.' 'Legislative enactments respecting tithes of a thousand years ago, are extant, but none that create the Tax.'*

Mother Church: " Without meaning to stop our friend, for it is well to have what is really stated

---

* 'Church Property, what it is, and whose,' by Wm. Best, a Baptist Minister, pp. 7, 8.

fairly brought before us, perhaps it may be convenient to make a remark or two upon the words just read. We have already discussed the difference between Parliament having the power, and the right to do anything; and I think we are pretty well agreed, as all honest Englishmen will be, that the power of Parliament ought only to be exercised in doing that which is right. And it would certainly not be right, but wrong and unjust to attempt to alter the doctrines, disciplines, or ceremonies of the Church, in opposition to the Church, or only to please a small section; or even a few enemies of the Church, and would certainly lead to a serious breach if persisted in."

"Then there is another point named, which is designed to tell against the Church, but which really much strengthens our position, when fully looked into, and will appear on the very face of it, when once named. It is said that 'the claim to tithes is a claim at common law,'—'that our Clergy have no claim for tithe except that which they derive from the law of the land.' 'That legislative exactments respecting tithes of a thousand years ago are extant, but none that create the tax.' Well now, we freely and willingly admit all this, except the word *tax*, for it is inapplicable; tithes are not a tax, but the payment of a just demand, like rents of land. But we can have no better security or guarantee for the validity of our tithe than that of the *common law* or the *law of the land*, or *the legislative enactments respecting tithes of a thousand years ago.* For the common law is the basis of all our other laws, that which has been upheld through ages past, and has come down to us as the settlement of our forefathers in the land. 'It is a name given to it,' says Judge Blackstone (Vol. 1 p. 85) 'in contradistinction to other laws, as the statute law, the civil law, the law of merchants, and the like; or more probably as a law common to all the realm, the *jus commune* or *folcright* mentioned by King Edward, the elder, after the abolition of the several provincial customs and particular laws before mentioned.' The right of the Church to her property, then, stands upon the same footing, by their own confession, as the validity of a deed in law to property when properly sealed and delivered; it stands on the same footing as that law whereby the eldest son alone is heir to his ancestors; as that whereby money lent upon bonds is recoverable by action of debt; for all these as Blackstone further remarks, are doctrines, that are not set down in any written statute or ordinance, but depend merely upon immemorial usuage, that is, upon common law, for their support. I do not see therefore how we can have a stronger foundation upon which the Church can rest her claims and right to her property. It is one of the most ancient acknowledged rights of the land; an inheritance or freehold in property, as valid and settled as that of the landlord, and often more so. And it is difficult to see what impression our adversaries meant to convey to the minds of the people by such expressions as they use, unless they designed them to understand, that it was an unjust and improper thing to have the payment of tithes enforced by the law of the land, and that the support which the civil power gives to recover them in case of refusal should be withdrawn, so as to leave it a voluntary action in all instance."

John Bull: "This is what, I think, they mean to imply, for I notice in another of their papers that they say '*It is the enforcement of that payment by the State*, which deprives it of its beauty and value, and which constitutes public endowment.' The words I have emphazized are printed in italics in the paper from which I read; and so also are the words upon which I shall lay some stress in the following quotation, given in another paper I have, which has been taken from the

Encyclopedia published by the Society of which Lord Brougham was President: and as it directly bears upon the question, I will read it to you. 'The Church relied upon the example of the Jews, and *required* a tenth to be paid. Meanwhile, the conversion of temporal princes to Christianity, and their zeal in favour of the new faith enabled the Church to obtain *the enactment of civil laws to compel* the payment of tithes. In England, the first instance of the law for the offering of tithes was that of Offa, King of Mercia, towards the end of the 8th century. He first gave the Church a civil right in tithes, and enabled the Clergy to recover them as their *legal* due by the *coercion of the civil power*. The law of Offa was at a later period extended to the whole of England by King Ethelwulph.' Article Tithes. And there is another quotation which is given from Burns in his Ecclesiastical laws, much to the same effect."

Mother Church: "The quotation you have just read gives, I allow, a very fair account of the matter, and I would accept it. It is clear also that it is this enforcement of payment, this coercion of the civil power, which they desire to hold up to reprobation, so as to make it offensive in the eyes of the people, in order to get Parliament to withhold its support, and the protection of this right to the Church. But I want you all particularly to notice, that it is because the tithes are a most just, settled, and valid claim upon the property, just as much as the landlord's rent, that *there are enactments of civil law to compel the payment*, and that they can be recovered as *a legal due by the coercion of the civil powers*. And if they had not been just and right, well settled and valid claims, the law would not have upheld and maintained them. Moreover, the Parochial tithes are not, I maintain, the product of the public law in the main, *much less exclusively*, as I trust convincingly to shew you ; but, that the public law was rather the product or result of those who had the right to give and to perpetuate tithes : and this is especially to be noticed in Ethelwulph's charter. The public law is not usually arbitrarily imposed upon the nation; and, in this case *it was evidently made in obedience to the pious impulses*, in the main, of those to whom the property chiefly belonged ; and no one will dispute, but that they had a right to make the payment obligatory, even as people can now make payments obligatory, as a charge upon their own property. And the continual renewal of the law for many hundred years afterwards shows that it was regarded as a just right, and most acceptable to the nation in general; though there would be those who would try to evade paying tithes, as they do now. See you not then, how this very view, which they have brought forwards, to damage us in the eyes of the people, is one that very much strengthens the value of our cause. Their design in this savours of that base method, which is sometimes adopted, to wet the appetite of the multitude by pandering to their lust for plunder in some shape. They might as well object to pay landlords' rents, as not to pay tithes, and make the obtaining of rents as objectionable to the people, *because there are enactments of the civil law to compel the payment, and because they can be recovered as a legal due by the coercion of the civil power.* It may be a pleasing doctrine to advocate, to those who have to pay rents and tithes ; and there is the prospect held out to the mass of somehow getting a share of the plunder, and being benefited by a general kind of hotch-potch of property. Every honest mind, however, will repudiate the doctrine or sentiment as most dishonest and pernicious: and it will only be received and entertained in minds that have become depraved, and lost to a true sense of what is right and wrong. But do not let me detain our friend, Mr.

Bull, from giving us some further quotations from the statements of those who are seeking to rob me; as it is only fair to hear what they say, and to listen to their arguments in favour of their scheme."

John Bull : " I am almost ashamed of producing them, after what you have said, my venerable Lady, for you have shewn very clearly that the Church has a right to her property; but there is another doctrine or notion which they have broached, which for consumate impudence, if not for something else I could name, beats everything I ever heard. Here it is, 'We are told that the Church has an indefeasible right to such and such property : that tithes and glebes and other endowments belong to the Church, and it really seems to be supposed that such phrases convey a valid meaning. So far from this they are utterly meaningless. The Church of England does not, and cannot possess a rood of ground, nor any building, nor property of any kind. What is the Church of England ? We leave others to answer the question positively. We say negatively that it is not a corporation, and, therefore cannot hold property. . . . A Dean and Chapter is a corporation aggregate. A Bishop or Rector or Vicar, is a corporation sole. In these corporations, the freehold of Ecclesiastical property is vested.

The fee simple is, we are told in abeyance. It really lies with the people of England.' 'It will be seen then,' the writer continues, 'that the talk about such and such property belonging to the Church is without meaning. Property may be held by a natural person, by a man or a woman, but the Church is neither a man nor a woman. Property may be held by a political person, *i. e.*, by a corporation, but the Church of England is not a corporation. It does not and cannot possess property, and therefore cannot be despoiled of property. And what is the interest of a Bishop, or Rector, or Vicar, or of a Dean and the members of his chapter in Church property? A life interest—no more. If this is secured to him, he cannot be said to suffer any wrong, whatever may be the fate of the Church property. Now it is very obvious that a corporation is a fictitious person,—a person created by the State and for public advantage. What the State has created it can also dissolve. It can dissolve any existing Ecclesiastical corporation. Such corporations have been dissolved, and without stretch of Governmental prerogative. And if Government has power to dissolve one it has power to dissolve all.' And again we have these words, 'who, then, or what is the Church of England? Our reply is the people of England, the whole of the people of England constitute the Church of England. The Church of England is the people of England, Ecclesiastically considered. And if they concur in such a measure of dissolution as I have supposed, who, I ask, would be spoliated? A man cannot rob himself, neither can a nation."* Mr. Bull then continued, "this is pretty strong language, but I thought you had better hear some of their keenest words. What do you think of them?"

The Old Lady of Threadneedle Street, here said: "If I may be allowed to speak, it appears to me the words you have read are an utter confusion of right and wrong; a most dangerous and deceptive way of talking or writing; just so much truth on the surface as to gild over the wrong or untruth, so as to make it appear right. There is a smattering of truth and a smattering of learning, but much false logic and foolish twaddle! The whole of the people of England *do not* constitute the Church of England. Every one, even the children in our national schools can see this. Dissenters are not members of the Church of England. The Baptists, the Independents, the Quakers and Romanists are not belonging to the Church of England, though

* 'Church Property, what is it, and whose?' p.p. 12, 13.

they are the people of England; they are separated from it, and form distinct bodies, outside the Church. Sometimes I find the opponents of the Church but too anxious to prove, when they had some object to serve or some point to gain, that there are almost as many Noncomformists of different bodies, distinct from the Church as there are members of the Church of England, so that it appears they can talk two ways. There was, I grant, a theory long ago advocated that all the people of England should belong to the Church of England, and attempts were made to compel them by the State; for the idea was to regard the whole as one family, with the King as the father, as it were, who should direct and order all things for his subjects as his children, —but the theory and the attempts soon broke down. It could not, and did not, and does not exist. All the people of England do not belong to the Church of England."

"Then again, there is another fallacy in the words you have just read, Mr. Bull. As the Church of England certainly does not include all the people of England, so also the Church of England is not confined to the Bishops and Clergy of the Church, who mainly receive the endowments of the Church for the service they render.

This is another exploded error, out of which the adversaries of the Church try to make capital. There is, as is well known, a vast body of laypeople throughout the whole of England, to be found in every parish of the land, who belong to the Church of England, and form, with the Clergy, as truly and distinctly a religious body or society—as, and in one sense [more so than the Baptists or Independents. And it is for them— the *Laity* of the Church—that the services of the Bishops or Clergy who receive the endowments in the main, are required; and though a life interest be secured to the Bishops and Clergy, the Deans and their Chapters, yet, I ask, is the vast, important, and influential body of Church-people, to be set on one side and not considered? Have not they an interest for themselves and their children, that the services of the Church should be continued to future generations? Or are these rights of Church-people to be ignored, and are these services to come to an end, or be very inadequately maintained, as first one and then another of the Bishops and of the Clergy die? Is it not a monstrous proposition? cruel, as it is unjust, to keep the Laity of the Church out of the question as having no rights; and, to make it out that they have no interest in the endowments being continued to the Church, is absurd and ridiculous!"

"You, venerable Lady," turning to Mother Church, "have shewn the specious sophistry of the argument that because Parliament has the power to confiscate any property in the land it has the right, for this would make Parliament have the right to do wrong. But before I conclude what I have to say, there is another matter in which the words which Mr. Bull has just read to us are at fault; alluding to the Dean and the Chapter being a corporation aggregate, and the Clergyman being a corporation sole, they can have no right in the property of the Church beyond a life interest, it is also stated that when the Clergyman dies it ceases to belong to the Church, and should revert to the State. This, I take to be the point of the argument. But is not the reverse of this the true statement of the question. Is not the Clergyman a Corporation sole and the Dean and Chapter a Corporation aggregate, *in order that the property may be continued to the Church for the benefit of the parishioners in perpetuity*; and does not this instrument or process of the law prevent the property of the

Church passing out of her hands to others—
to either individuals or to the State?'"

"I do not wish you to depend upon my own
judgment alone in this question, and would refer
you again to what one of the most learned commentators of the English laws, Judge Blackstone,
says on the matters. (Book I., chap. xviii., pp.
469–470.) 'The first division of corporation is
into aggregate and sole. *Corporations aggregate*
consist of many persons united together into one
Society, and are kept up by a perpetual succession
of members, so as to continue for ever: of which
kind are the mayor and commonalty of a city,
the head and fellows of a college, the Dean and
Chapter of a Cathedral Church. *Corporations sole*
consist of one person only and his successors, in
some particular station, who are incorporated by
law, in order to give them some legal capacities
and advantages, *particularly that of perpetuity*,
which in their natural persons they could not
have had. In this sense the King is a sole corporation: so is a Bishop: so are Deans and Prebendiaries, distinct from their several Chapters:
and so is every Parson and Vicar. And the
necessity, or at least use, of this institution will
be very apparent, if we consider the case of a
Parson of a Church. At the original endowment

of Parish Churches, the freehold of the Church, the Church-yard, the Parsonage-house, the Glebe and Tithe of the Parish, were vested on the then Parson *by the bounty of the donor*, as a temporal recompense to him for his spiritual care of the inhabitants, and with intent that the same emoluments *should ever afterwards continue* as a recompense for the same care. But how was this to be effected? The freehold was vested in the Parson, and, if we suppose it vested in his natural capacity, on his death it might descend to his heir, and would be liable to his debts and incumbrances; or, at best, the heir might be compellable, at some trouble and expense, to convey these rights to the succeeding incumbent. The law, therefore, has wisely ordained that the parson, *quatenus* parson, shall never die, any more than the King; by making him and his successors a corporation. By which means all the original rights of the parsonage are preserved entire to the successors; for the present incumbent, and his predecessor who lived seven centuries ago, are in law one and the same person; and what was given to the one was given to the other also.'

"I think nothing can be more clear and decisive than these words of the learned judge, to shew that the present arrangement respecting the corporation sole and aggregate in the Church, is a most valuable instrument in the law for securing the property of the Church in tact for a perpetuity ; and that the arguments and assertions of the writer whom Mr. Bull has just quoted are utterly worthless and false; and designed to put men upon a wrong scent, or rather prejudice them to perpetrate a wrong against the Church."

Here a general desire was manifested to postpone their conference till the same day in the following week. Warm thanks were given to the last speaker, as it was felt she had cleared up several important points. The Old Lady of Threadneedle Street intimated that she had a few more words to say respecting the endowments of the Church, which she would reserve till their next meeting ; and as she did not think she should trespass upon the province Mother Church had marked out, she hoped their venerable friend would proceed with the promise of producing those proofs and evidences of the title-deeds of the Church so far as they were discoverable. This being again promised, they soon separated.

PART IV.

ON the same day, in the following week, the three venerable Ladies, with Mr. Bull, were again seated in conference.

Madam Britannia, turning towards the Lady from Threadneedle Street, said, "I believe, dear Madam, you purposed saying something further about the Endowments of the Church, when we parted last week, previous to our entering upon the consideration of the evidences and proofs of the title-deeds of the Church, which our venerable friend has promised to lay before us."

John Bull: "May I be excused if I first ask permission to read two or three more extracts, from the papers and little books which those who want to take away the property of the Church have put out, as they may serve to give point to our considerations upon this matter, especially as they seem to challenge any possibility of the Church being able to produce any vestige of evidence of her being voluntarily endowed."

Madam Britannia: "Oh, yes; by all means let us hear what they have to say." And turning to the other two ladies, she said, "I suppose it is agreeable to you that our friend, Mr. Bull, should do this."

The other two ladies assented; one of them saying, "Certainly; let us hear the utmost they can say, for we are fully prepared to meet any charge they may bring against the Church being voluntarily endowed; and, I think, we have nothing to fear from the most thorough investigation into the whole matter."

John Bull here got out his papers and little books, and said, "I shall not detain you long, as I shall only give you a few short extracts which I have marked, and which seem to give us the pith of their objections. In one of the papers I read, 'The theory of pious gifts we cannot understand—it is incredible.'*

'To us tithe, like income-tax, is known as a legal impost. It is claimed, and the claim is allowed and payment made, not in obedience to the intentions and gifts of mythical benefactors, in the dark ages, but in obedience to well known and compulsory law.' †

* 'Church Property: what is it, and whose?' p. 9.
† Ibid, p. 10.

Again, this writer tauntingly asks, 'Are not the lands that belong to the Church to be regarded as endowments created by private bounty? If so, let the deeds be shewn. Let us learn from them who gave—when the gifts were made—and for what purpose?'* As if he thought this could not be done. Another of the opponents of the Church seems to be of the same opinion also, for he says 'We have heard much talk about the pious ancestors who, in the good old times, gave the bulk of the property by which their denomination is supported. Let us have some of their names, and a quotation or two from their deeds.'† I will not now give you any more extracts, which are much to the same purport, as I am anxious to learn how these insinuations are to be met."

The Lady living in Threadneedle Street: "What I have to say further will not be wide of the mark which has been set out for this day's discussion; and will, I trust, prepare the way for what our venerable friend, Mother Church, has to say. All property comes to us in one of three ways, either by inheritance, by gift, or by purchase. It is true that those who have recently

* 'Church Property: what is it, and whose?' p. 13.
† Letters from Dissenting Ministers in newspapers, 1873.

purchased property can shew by their title-deeds from whom they have purchased it, and that those persons from whom they purchased it were able to give them a good title to it. Twenty-five, or thirty years' undisputed possession, is now, I believe, by Act of Parliament considered a sufficient title, and it is considered a very good title if undisputed possession can be traced back for fifty or sixty years : and further, there are some old families that can go back hundreds of years for their title; and it is usually considered that the further back they can go, to prove *the possession* of their property by regular descent, the more valid and indefeasible the title is. And yet how few of these persons can shew the *original* title-deeds or grants of the land which they own. Some may be able to go up to Henry VIII.'s time; fewer still to Edward I., and I doubt if any can go back with a veritable title-deed to the reign of William the Conqueror, when there was a fresh distribution of land in many instances. Nevertheless, the inability of owners to produce the original title-deeds of their property is no bar to their claim : their ancestors had formerly a pre-. scriptive right, which was sufficient, and the want of original deeds did not invalidate their right to the property, so long as they were able to trace their title by other means. And in like manner I hold, that though my venerable friend here could not show any documents or title-deeds of the original donations of land to prove by what means, and as to how, she came into her property in various instances, yet the length of time which, in every instance, she has held possession and had the use and advantages of the property, undoubtedly gives her a prescriptive right to it in common law, as it does in like cases of property where the owners have no proof of the original grant of their property."

John Bull: "A prescriptive right is, I understand, properly applied to property where the title-deeds of ownership are not forthcoming; nevertheless, where the original grant from the Crown or otherwise is lost, there are, in almost all cases now, deeds to show how the present owners have come into possession of their lands. In cases of purchase, they can show how they obtained the property from those who had an acknowledged, if not undisputed, right to it; and in case of inheritance or bequest, there are the wills of the former owners, or the baptismal registers and other evidences, to show how the present owners are validly entitled to their several possessions. And these are acknowledged as good proofs of the owners' titles, in law."

The Lady from Threadneedle Street : "Just so; and there is something analagous to this in the inheritance of all Church property, which it is desirable to notice, and which in the eyes of the law is recognized as equally valid. There is, I believe, in most parishes, a book or roll called *the Terrier*, often written on parchment, giving a description of the lands and emoluments belonging to the Living, which is for the benefit and support of the Vicar or Rector, as the case may be, who is appointed to serve the cure. There are thousands of these Terriers scattered up and down the country, in the several parishes; and in most cases they go back hundreds of years to prove the right of the Church, in these several places, to the property which she possesses. These, therefore, I assert, on behalf of my friend, to be most valid and indefeasible Title-deeds to the property she owns. Besides this, in the Register Courts of every Diocese, there is a record made of each succeeding Vicar or Rector, to the various Livings in the Dioceses; going back here also, in most instances, hundreds of years, and proving a constant succession of persons with acknowledged titles to the possession and enjoyment of these several endowments. And these persons, as we have seen from Judge Blackstone's work, are accounted in law as the lawful inheritors of the lands and emoluments, just as much as the eldest son is accounted the heir to his father's property, and proves, by his baptismal register and other collateral evidences, that he is entitled to possession. The fact of these several Clergymen being duly entered upon the Diocesan register, as succeeding the former holders of these several possessions, is a sufficient and satisfactory evidence,—its being at the time the then living Bishop's guarantee,—that such several persons were lawfully appointed; and consequently, lawfully entitled to the benefits of the Livings to which they were appointed.

"Furthermore, there are in every parish register-books of Burials, Baptisms, and Marriages, in which the Vicars or Rectors of these parishes have subscribed their names, time after time, and in constant succession, as they have followed one another for hundreds of years. This is a further collateral evidence that they were holding such office, and in possession of the emoluments attached thereto, and that their holding and enjoyment of the livings also, were acknowledged and maintained in law."

Madam Britannia: "You have certainly furnished us already with sufficient proofs, and even Title-deeds, or what are tantamount thereto, of the Church's right to her property. Documents, deeds, and registers, which, if collected from the various parishes of England, would require a great many waggons to convey them. And you have put the matter so clearly before us, that I can scarce conceive that other evidence were needed of the validity of the Church's right to her possessions. Still, whilst we are examining the matter, we shall be glad to hear what our venerable Friend has to say further upon the question, and to receive the evidence which, I believe, she is prepared to give."

Mother Church: "I shall be most happy to do so, and to add what confirmation I can give to prove that the Church has a real title to her property; but, I must first of all tender my sincere thanks to my excellent friend, for the very able and valuable evidence which she has produced in support of my right to the property I possess; for she has undoubtedly shewn, independently of the evidences I may be able to bring before you, that the Church has a valid title, and that her property is secured to her by law, in the best possible manner in which any property can be secured to any one. Overthrow the right of the Church to her property, and you can overthrow that of any other in the land.

"But now, as you may surmise from what I have said, there is other evidence to produce relative to the Church's title to her property. The endowments, as you are aware, are chiefly of two kinds, viz., *Lands* which have been given to the Church, and the *Tithes*, or what are now called Tithe rent-charges upon land. Let us take these separately.

"First, as to the landed property of the Church. It has been shewn that there are many owners of property who cannot trace the title of their property back very far,—many not a hundred years; and very few to any *original* grant or bequest before the Reformation; and it is of course not to be expected that the Church should be able to show, in all cases, how she at first came into possession of her property, or who were the original donors; bearing in mind, however, what my worthy friend has said, as to the manner in which Church property can be traced back hundreds of years, we are further enabled to afford you *proofs*, in many instances, *as to who gave the property to the Church in certain places: the time when it was thus given:* and *the very names, and description of the properties, with the acreage or extent, that were thus given.* And if I prove these points in abundant number of cases, as I am prepared to do, then I must contend that it affords a presumptive evidence that other lands, now in the Church's possession, have, in the majority of cases, been thus originally given, and that voluntarily, or that the lands have been purchased by the voluntary offerings of Churchmen, though we cannot pretend, at this remote period of time, in such cases to give the names of the donors, or how the property came into the Church's possession, or to specify the exact time when the property was thus given or acquired. For the people of England have in past generations been as keenly alive to keeping hold of what was their own, as people are now; and it is impossible to conceive that the Church could have obtained the possession of these lands or tenements, and have held undisputed possession of them for so many years past, if they had not had a good right and legitimate title to them."

"In direct reply, however, to the taunts which have been thrown out against us, respecting the Church acquiring possession of the property, when they ask, 'give us some of their names and a quotation or two from their deeds,' referring to the Donors of property and their gifts, we have but simply to answer,—here they are. Now the proofs I can bring are of such a considerable extent, and so very numerous, that I fear I shall take up too much of your valuable time, and weary you too much with them, unless I endeavour to make some selection of them, during various periods of time, and condense the evidence as much as possible, but still, at the same time, thoroughly to convince you of its authenticity, and satisfy you that there is very much more of such evidence forthcoming, if any one will be at the trouble to examine it fully.

"I shall not now revert to any property acquired by the Church within the last two hundred and thirty or forty years. This must be considered afterwards by itself. There is ample evidence to shew what property the Church then possessed in various places—at, and before, the time I have named,—and how she came into possession of it in many instances.

"Let us take one Diocese alone, as an example of what may be found in others; and we take that of London, as one that is most known to the largest number of people. In 'Newcourt's Repertorium,' which consists of two large folio volumes, the Diocese of London, as it formerly existed, including parts of Hertfordshire and Buckinghamshire as well as Middlesex, is only considered. In these volumes we have numberless instances given of the names of donors, and the donations given to the several Churches, both long before the Reformation, and since then down to A.D. 1636, at which time the value of the endowments in every parish, then existing, is given; and, when these several endowments are named, we are told also from what they were derived or in what they consist, and the exact amount under several heads,—so much from this source and so much from another—in each case, at this time. Moreover, the names are given too of the various Vicars and Rectors who succeeded to these Livings, for hundreds of years back, extending to a long time before the Reformation. The volumes are full of condensed information on these matters,—information which was well known at the time, and could be tested as to its truthfulness. As examples, however, of donors' names and gifts, of lesser value to what I have yet to shew you, I have culled out a few instances from a few pages to illustrate the rest. In most of the cases I name other endowments had previously existed.

St. Christopher's Rectory, on the north side of Threadneedle-street. Richard Sherington (who died A.D. 1392), and John Clavering (who died A.D. 1421), both gave lands to this church.—Mr. John Kendrick, citizen and draper, of London, (who dwelt in the parish and was buried in the church,) A.D. 1624, gave £2,400 to the Draper's Company to purchase lands of the yearly value of £400 for charitable purposes, among which £20 was to go for ever to the curate of St. Christopher's to read divine service in the said Parish Church at six o'clock in the morning, every day in the week, for ever.—Two or three others gave endowments to the Church in Edward III. reign and afterwards, viz: Thomas Legg, John Watley, and John Gedney.—Mr. Benedict Harlewing gave certain tenements in Fleet-street, now let on lease: £20 per annum of which is set for reading prayers every day of the week at six o'clock in the evening.

St. Michael's Royal.
This Church, with a College attached thereto, was built and endowed by Sir Richard Whitington, several times Mayor of London, the last whereof was in the year 1418. He made provision for a Master, who was to be the Rector, and for four fellows, M.A., and for clerk and choristers.
—A. D. 1481, Gelbert Heydock, Doctor in Divinity, gave 600 marks to found two Chaplaincies : the amount, however, by some means, fell short, and only one was founded.

Alhallows, Barking.
—In the year 1295, Adam Blakeney endowed this Church with five marks per annum.
—In Edward III. reign it was further endowed by John de Cambridge ; and further augmented, by one Godwyn Turke, to six marks per annum.
—In the year 1388 John Crolys and Thomas Pike gave further endowments.

Alhallows Less, Curacy.
—In 20 Richard II. reign, Philip S. Clere gave two messuages to this Church.
—In 1562, Mrs. Elizabeth Bannister, by deed dated Sept. 24, in this year, gave Five Pounds per annum for twelve sermons to be preached in this Church.
—In the year 1624 Roger Daniel left by will Eight Pounds per annum.

St. Bennet, Grace Church.
—In 20 Elizabeth : One Robert Offley, the elder, gave by Indenture, a tenement.
—In the year 1610 William Jordan gave another tenement.
—In the year 1605, Mrs. Doxie, widow, left by will Fifty Pounds, " for purchasing the yearly value of 50s., to be paid yearly to the parson of this parish, and his successors for ever, for his better maintenance ; provided he be resident and preach every Sabbath-day, within this Parish Church."
—In the year 1631 Mrs. Joan Newton, widow, left by will Thirty Pounds for the maintenance of a Lecturer in this Church.

Such are a sample of what are to be found in the volumes. And abundant more instances might be produced if needed.

And though the lands, tenements, and leases herein named, may appear of small amount, we must remember that this said property has risen enormously in value, so as now to be of great worth. But I suppose there can be no reasonable objection to the Church enjoying the increased value of her property, as others do."

" Let me however give you another cluster of

endowments to the Church in various parishes, in a condensed form, as given by Archdeacon Lyall, of Colchester, in one of his charges to the clergy, containing several instances of Livings that had been endowed within his Archdeaconry.

'*Audley*, endowed by Robert de Ram, in the reign of King Stephen : *Ashdon*, endowed in the reign of William the First, by Gaufredus and Randulphus Baynard : *Great Badfield*, in 1090, by Gilbert de Clare : *Great Bentley*, about the same time, by Aberic de Vere : *Great Clacton*, by Richard de Beauvys, or de Beloncis : *Coggeshall*, by Earl Godwin (with the tithes of Sisted) in the time of Edward the Confessor : *Elsenhem*, by Beatrix de Say in 1200 : *White Notley*, by Roger Bigod, in the reign of William the First : *Black Notley*, by Walter de Mandeville, in 1218 : *Rickling*, by Geoffry de Say, in the reign of Henry the Second : *Weeley*, by Elgiva, a noble Saxon lady, in the time of Edward the Confessor. It would be easy,' adds the Archdeacon, 'to extend the number of examples ; and even to produce the very words of the endowments, many of which are given at length by Newcourt.'*

* See 'Blunt's Essays.' VIII. p. 349.

Such is the very kind of evidence, I think, which has been demanded by our opponents, and required from us as a defiant test of our title,— and here we have instances of them, in large abundance, especially when you consider that I have only given you a few instances out of one Diocese alone. And I would only just add, under this head, that if similar volumes of other Dioceses were compiled and taken in connection with the kind of evidence set forth by my worthy friend, as shown in the Terriers of Parishes, and in the Diocesan and Parochial Registers, as to the constant succession of the clergy of the Church, who, for their services, have enjoyed the emoluments of their several livings, I cannot but think that the proofs in support of the Church's title to the said property are most abundant, as well as conclusive and indisputable."

Madame Britannia : " This is certainly evidence that will strengthen your cause; and I must candidly confess that I am gratified to see you able to bring forward such proofs as you have done, and such as, I think, ought to set this vexed question at rest, as it is a sufficient answer to the interrogations of your opponents."

Mother Church : " I am pleased to hear this

from you ; for it encourages me to proceed in the very arduous task I have undertaken. I would willingly have been quiet, and given my whole time and attention to the other important duties that I have to perform; but I felt that vast interests, not only as concerning myself but many others, depended upon setting this matter in a full and fair manner before you and the public, that I felt compelled to undertake this defence ; and shall now, with your leave,. proceed with my cause."

"We are able to go, even much further back still, than such instances as I have already given you, for evidences of voluntary offerings to the Church,—to a still more remote. period, and in many instances to a time before the parochial system became established in this country. On the first planting of Christianity in England, many noble gifts were made to the Church ; and the zeal and devotion of the early converts to Christianity in this country seemed to exceed that of other nations. At first the *Diocese* was as one large parish, with the Bishop at its head; and after a Diocese had been created, it was not long before the Bishop and his zealous Clergymen endeavoured to establish a Monastery, and other religious houses, for the nurturing of the religious life, for obtaining better instruction and religious education than could be obtained in the world during that unsettled age, and for training a native ministry, so that the Bishop might have a constant succession of educated clergy to send out into various parts of his Diocese to preach the Gospel to the people."

John Bull: "Perhaps you will excuse me just making one remark at this point, and it is this: that I do not think that Monasteries, and such like places, are looked upon with much favour by the majority of the religious people in England now."

Mother Church: "I agree with you, and it is not without some good reason that they have been led to view them with some disfavour. But the Monasteries and other religious houses of the Ancient British and Anglo-Saxon Churches were very different to what they afterwards became under papal domination. They were more like the schools of the Prophets, when Samuel and Elijah were at their head; or like the Missionary stations or centres which the late Bishop [Gray] of Capetown was so anxious to establish, as the best means for establishing the gospel of Christ in a large tract of the country. Only those anciently established were much larger and better supported and endowed. Those belonging to them lived hard, laborious, pious, and useful lives. Many barren tracts of land around them were brought into a high state of cultivation by them. The services of God were constantly and most devoutly performed. They were under the direction of the Bishop of the Diocese, and much fostered by him, for they were a great help to him in furthering the promotion of Christianity; and men from all the country round would flock to them, from time to time, and would be kindly and hospitably entertained whilst they were more perfectly instructed in the truth of Christ and His salvation; and many noble persons, when weary of the world, would in the latter days of their life retreat to them altogether, that they might the better prepare for another world; and in many instances left noble gifts to these Monasteries and religious houses. The places are not, therefore, to be judged by what they afterwards became in popish hands."*

* Soames, in his History of the Anglo-Saxon Church, says, "Other facilities for spreading religion, and secular information also, were now generally provided by means of Monasteries. Rarely was a Prince converted, or awakened to a serious concern

"I have alluded to these places as great centres of Church life and work, in those early days of Christianity in this country, because we have many instances of liberal benefactions made to

for eternity, without signalizing his altered state by one or more of these foundations. This munificence was highly beneficial to society. An age of barbarism and insecurity required such cloistered retreats for nurturing, concentrating, and protecting the peaceful luminaries of learning and religion. From the convent-gate, heralds of salvation went forth to evangelize the country," pp. 96, 97. See also Bede IV. 27, pp. 348, 349.

Again Soames says, "England, it is true, was early and abundantly supplied with conventual foundations, liberally endowed. But these were generally rather Colleges than regular Monasteries. In them were provided accommodation for ordinary Clergymen, education for youth, and a home for some few ascetics bound by solemn vows. . . . But England, probably, had never offered, in societies exclusively and uniformly ascetic, any sufficient facilities for nurturing such a disposition. The munificence which had consecrated so many spots by religious houses, appears, indeed, usually to have been stimulated by palpable deficiencies of religious instruction. In raising and endowing a *Minster*, the vernacular form of *Monasterium*, Anglo-Saxon piety had apparently little else in view than a church for ordinary worship, surrounded by a body of Clergy, who might both serve it and itinerate in the neighbourhood. Eventually many of these establishments became Monasteries, in the sense affixed to that word by after ages. But one part of the generation, witnessing this change, condemned it as an injustice based upon delusion. The other part, probably, thought not of inquiring into the truth of such a change. . . . Innovations upon established usage and vested interests require, however, time and perseverance. A complete monastic triumph was accordingly delayed until after the Norman Conquest." Soames pp. 166, 167. See also, Inett. I. 329.

Waddington also, who enters fully into the abuses that crept into Monasteries, says, "In early ages the Monks were the subjects, and, as it were, the army of the Bishops." "Absolute exemptions from Episcopal authority were for some time rare."

them of which I desire you to take notice. I have selected a few for your consideration.

Glastonbury Abbey or Monastery.

A.D. 601. King Dammonia gave lands containing five families (quinque Cassata).*

—A.D. 675. Kenwalch bestowed Farramore, and other possessions upon it.

—A.D. 680. Kentwyn gave to it the manor of West Montaton, and Kenewalla bestowed some lands upon the monks also.

—King Ina was a great benefactor. He not only rebuilt the Abbey, but bestowed upon them the Manors of Brent, Lowry, and Poulton.

—Ethelard gave liberally, and Cuthred bestowed three hydes of land at Ure. And Kenwulf bestowed five hydes† upon them at a place called

---

But "finally the whole monastic body acknowledged no other dependence than on the Pope alone." And "during the eleventh, twelfth, and thirteenth centuries, the Holy See derived great power from the sort of separate hierarchy thus established."— Waddington's History of the Church, pp. 411, 412.

* The *familia* or *Cassate* seems to have been a circuit of ground sufficient for the maintenance of a family, and the cultivation by a plough, averaging from a hundred to one hundred and fifty acres

† A hide of land was not derived, as Polydore Virgil fancies, from the hide of a beast, as if an English hide of land were like the extent of Carthage, "Quantum taurino possint circundare tergo," but from the Saxon *hyd*, a house or habitation, from *Hydan* to cover. The quantity of a hyde was never expressly determined. *Gervase* of *Tilbury* makes it one hundred acres. The *Malmesbury* MSS., cited by Spelman, computes it at 96 acres, or four virgates : every virgate being 24 acres.

Wadaton, and other possessions at Huneresbury. There are other gifts to this place, but these must suffice.*

Evesham. A.D. 709. Kenredus, and Offa, governor of East Angles, endowed this Abbey with large possessions.

—During the time Egwin was Bishop of Worcester, 22 towns were gained to the Monastery.†

Croyland, or Crudeland, raw and muddy, which the Monks reclaimed and cultivated, had many benefactions made to it. Among others, one Turketellus, Chancellor to King Edred, was the greatest benefactor to the place. He redeemed their lands, and endowed the place with no less than *sixty Manors.*

A.D. 975. The Monastery was said to be worth £10,000, which in those days was a large sum.

A.D. 1000. Osketulus, a person of great quality, was a considerable benefactor.‡

Winchester. King Alfred designed to build and endow a new Minster at this place, but death prevented his carrying out his pious design, and long cherished wish. We are, however, further told that for the more solemn carrying out of

* Dr. Hearne's History of Glastonbury, pp. 21, 23.
† Dr. Hearne's Leland, vol. 6, p. 158.
‡ Dr. Hearne's Leland, vol. 6., p. 160.

Alfred's plan and injunctions, a great council was convened at Winchester. King Edward's first inclination, it is said, was to found the new Monastery out of the property belonging to the Church of St. Swithun, but he was otherwise advised by Grimald. "God," said the venerable priest, "will not accept robbery for burnt offering." A large and liberal foundation was then determined upon. Many of the Magnates and Clergy offered their contributions for its endowment. And within two years the new and stately Abbey was built and decorated.*

"This certainly shews that they both understood and acted on the voluntary principle in those early times."

"I have more to say about the endowments of the Church at Winchester, but I would here advert, for a while, to the will of King Alfred. He died A.D. 901. After bequeathing large portions of property, which are named, to Edward, his eldest son (my yldiste sone), and lesser portions to his oldest daughter (ilderyst dowther), to his brother, and brother's son, his cousin, and various other persons named, he gives to the Archbishop of Canterbury an hundred marks, and the

* Liber Monasterii De Hyda, Edwards, Intro. xxvii.

same to Esne, Bishop of Hereford, and to Werfertha, Bishop of Worcester, and to Asser, Bishop of Sherbourne. And two hundred and fifty pounds to fifty priests, and fifty shillings (schilyngs) to every one of God's servants."

"I have brought the terms of this great king's will before you, however, not so much for the sake of mentioning the sums granted to the ministers of the Church, but for you to observe that the kings of those days had their own private property, and could point it out by name; and though they were probably among the largest landowners of the nation, yet in giving to the Church they gave from what was really and specially their own, and not what belonged to the nation."

"But to continue the endowments to the Church at Winchester, Edward the Elder, as he was called, to distinguish him from Edward the Confessor, granted, at various times between the first and twenty-first year of his reign, several lands to this new Minster, comprising the Manors of Micheldever, Anne, Caudover, Durley, and Thorley in Hampshire; and those of Cranbourne, Collingbourne, and Chiseldon in Wiltshire.*

* Liber Monasterii De Hyda, Edwards, p. 333.

—By the year 924 it is computed that New Minster owned nearly 17,000 acres of land in Hampshire, and 10,800 in Wiltshire.

Several Kings, Noblemen, and Priests, after this time, made further grants of land to this Monastery, three or four instances of which I will here give you."

1st. Bishop Ælfsige's bequest; between A.D. 925 and 940. And we have the very words given in his Will respecting the lands he gave; which are, when put into readable English, "I grant "the land of Crondall to Ælfheah, and after "his life let it go to the Old Monastery at Win-"chester. And I give to my nephew the land at "Anne; and after his life to the New Monastery "at Winchester. And the land at Titchbourne "to Wlfric Cufing, and after his life to the Old "Monastery. And the land at Ringwood to the "Old Monastery." *

2nd. "I, Ethelnoth, a priest, give the land at "Basing to the New Monastery to enjoy it for "ever."
This is witnessed by the King and two Bishops.

3rd. Ethelner, an Alderman or Earl, gave by will, also, to the New Monastery at Winchester, a hundred mancuses of gold, and thirteen hides

* Liber Monasterii De Hyda. Edwards p. 343.

K

of land—those which Lufa held; "and this I "bought," he says, "of my lord, when it fell into "his hands. And I give the lands of Tidworth "to my wife for her life, and after her life let it "go to the place where I rest."

4th. We then find that King Edred A.D. 951-5? gives by Will to the Old Monastery of Winchester three towns, Diontune, and Domerham, and Calne. Furthermore, he granteth to the new Monastery at Winchester three towns, that is to say, Wharewel, and Andever, and Clere. And he granteth to the nunne Minster of Myncheus three towns, Selborn, and Hamme, and Bradford. He also granteth to the nunne Minster at Chester thirty pounds, and to Wyltone thirty pounds, and thirty pounds to Schaftysbury.

Also he giveth to the Archbishop of Christchurch (Erchebyschop of Crystys-chyrche) four hundred pounds, to rejoice the time of his life, and then it is to go to the Minster of Christchurch, Canterbury.

He also bequeaths (beqweythyth) to Elphege, and to the Bishops of Winchester, four hundred pounds; also to Osketyl Bishop, and the Monks of Dorchester, four hundred pounds, and then to the Bishops' see as before bequeathed. Also to Wlfhelm Bishop four hundred pounds; and then to all the other Diocesan Bishops an hundred handfuls of Gold.*

Such were some of the munificent gifts to the Church in those early days of the Church in this country.

It is interesting to note further, and it will help to confirm our cause, if we mention the facts, that having suffered much loss and persecution at Winchester, several of the Monks migrated, in Henry I.'s reign, to the extensive plain called Hyde Mead, from which the Abbey here built was named. Here they flourished for a time; but living in the days of the Norman Kings and Norman Bishops, who ravaged the Church, their Abbey was burnt down, and much property wrested from them. And in the year 1311 Bishop Wodelock issued his Episcopal letters, reciting, "that part of the Monastery still lay in ruins, and that the Estates were insufficient for its complete restoration, and for the maintenance of due hospitality; commending to the faithful the good work of charitable assistance, and directing that collections should be made to that end in all the churches of his Diocese." †

* Liber Monasterii De Hyda. Edwards p. 155.
†Liber Monasterii de Hyda, Edwards, Intro. II. And Registrum de Wodelock, MS., Winch. fol. 165.

Here we have an instance again of a system of voluntary contributions, much after the fashion of the present day.

I shall now give you a few more instances;—I do not wish unnecessarily to multiply them, but it is only by dwelling upon this kind of evidence that you and the public will gain any adequate idea of the extensive character of the Church endowments in this country, in earlier days.

Waltham Abbey, was built and endowed by Harold, A.D. 1062, with a Dean and eleven secular Canons. In Henry II. reign they were, however, increased to twenty four, and then the foundation was changed into regular Canons.†

I want you particularly to note the character of this change, which took place in this, and many other Monasteries, about this time, *i.e.*, after the period of the Conquest under papal domination. The Canons Secular, or Parochial Clergy, were then ousted out of their places which they had in them; and the Canons Regular, as they were called, or the regular Monks, who were vehement supporters of the Pope, and so often opposed and oppressed the Parochial Clergy, were introduced into their places. Moreover, the Pope granted

* Hearne's Leland, vol. vi., p. 198.

these Monks exemption from the jurisdiction of the Bishop of the Diocese, and made them subject to himself only, or to those he appointed. But more of this, if time permit, afterwards.

Ramsay. This Abbey was founded A.D. 969, by Ailwine, Earl of East Angles, at the instigation of Oswald, Archbishop of York.*

Coventry. The Church in this place was plentifully endowed with lands and revenues by Leofric, Earl of Chester, and Godiva, his wife.†

Now one more instance of this kind and I will proceed to another point.

Ely. King Edgar, A.D. 960, granted forty hides of land, at Hatfield, to the Monastery at this place, together with the village of Dereham, in Norfolk.

—Bishop Ethelwold procured five more hides of land for it, at Meldeburne; three and a half hides at Earningeford, and twelve hides at Northwalde. It does not say how they were procured, but probably by the abundant alms of the faithful.

—The Lady of Ælftreda is also said to have given five hides at Holand in Essex.

—Other lands, which are named, were about this time purchased for the Monastery, by money which had been given.

* Hearne's Leland, vol. vi., p. 198.
† Ibid.

—One Godwin (*cir. A.D.* 1000) gave the village of Hoo.

—And Elmer, Godwin's brother, gave an estate at Hecham.

—Large possessions also were given to the Monastery by Leofwin, son of Adulf. These were the lands of Cingestune, the Rodings, and Undelcia; lands in Lackinghethe, Withleseye, Esteric, and Cotenham; an estate in London, afterwards called Abbotts-haie; Glamesford; the fisheries at Upstane, and an annual rent at Hadfield.

—Other benefactors about this time are also named: such were Etheliva and Elfwara, two Saxon ladies; Duke Brithnot; Ethelfleda; Uva; Oswi; Ederic, and many others.

" I would only now say that this is not a tithe of the evidence that could be produced; there are numerous sources from whence more can be brought, if it were called for, but it would occupy several days to go even cursorily over it, and I think I shall only be consulting your convenience not to go further into the evidences of this sort which I am ready to produce."

The others all agreed that it was needless to go further in bringing more instances of the kind forward, as they were amply satisfied with what they had heard, to convince them of the reality of the early endowments of the Church, and that these endowments did not come from the nation in its corporate capacity, but from the voluntary offerings and bequests of Church-people long ago.

Mother Church : " I would now, however, beg leave to *put in evidence* the Records of the Doomsday-Book. These records will serve to corroborate much of what I have already advanced, and being compiled by civil authority it is a kind of evidence independent of Ecclesiastical and other statements, that might be thought too favourable to the Church. The Book is, as it were, an independent witness of great weight; and should not be withheld from giving evidence on this occasion."

Madam Britannia : " Certainly not! A more ancient collection of documents of national importance and authority we could not have, and one upon the whole that is to be thoroughly relied upon. They form a Book that was drawn up by order of William the Conqueror, containing a survey of all the lands in England, except the three most Northern Counties, as the basis from which judgment was to be given, as to the tenures, value, and services therein described. It was completed in the year A.D. 1086.

But I am anxious that you should produce your witness."

Mother Church : " What you have stated respecting the Doomsday-Book is, I believe, correct. It was begun A.D. 1082, and finished A.D. 1086, in the 20th year of the reign of William I. And in the survey that was taken of all the land, those lands which belonged to the Church in various places are duly put down. And the fact of their being named and put down in this Book is a pretty good guarantee that they belonged to the Church ; and that they were acknowledged as such by the national officers appointed to look after this matter, and to return an accurate report."*

" I shall content myself, however, with giving

---

* The Royal Commissioners upon the oaths of the Sheriffs, the Lords of each Manor, the Presbyters of every Church, the Reeves of every Hundred, and six villanes of every Village, were to inquire into the name of the place, who held in Edward the Confessor's time, who was the present possessor, how many hides there were in the Manor, how many carucates in Demesno, how many Freemen, how many tenants in Soccage, how many in Villenage, how much wood, meadow, and pasture, how many mills and Fish-ponds, how much added and taken away, what the value, how much the tax in King Edward's time, what now, and what advance could be made upon it.

In the Doomsday-Book the Arable land was measured by carucates, the common Pasture land by hides, and the Meadow by acres. A carucate (from *caruca*, a plough) was one hundred and twenty acres up to one hundred and fifty.

you only *one example* of the account of lands belonging to the Church; and I think you will acknowledge that it is sufficient, though it is by no means the longest account, for, the survey of the several Manors of New minster, at *Winchester*, to which I have already drawn your attention, (the translation from the Doomsday-book) occupies several pages, viz., from page xcix. to cxiv.*

" In the return of lands as belonging to the *Abbey of Ely*, there were in *Hertfordshire* forty hides of land at Hadfield, five hides at Chelleselle, and four hides at Hadan. In *Cambridgeshire*, eight hides at Stovicesworde; three hides in Weslai; eight and a half hides at Waratinge; nine hides, forming the manor of Belesham; half a hide in Saham; five hides at Suafam; three hides and three virgates in Coeia; four and a half in Tuleberne; one hide and a half in Teversham. The manor of Horningesie, consisting of seven hides. One hide and a half in Wicheham, and a half in Berceham, and a half in Badburham. Two hides, three virgates and a half, in Pampesworde; ten acres attached to the same village; seven and a half hides and two acres in Trepeslaw. The Manor Havochestun, consisting of eight and a half hides, and one and a half in

* Doomsday-Book, fol. 59, verso, Col. 2.

Hurlestone. The Manor of Escelforde, consisting of nine hides and twenty four acres, with two and a half hides and nine acres in the same village held by Hardinius. The Manor of Stapleforde, consisting of ten hides, and two and a half hides in Wadone. One virgate in Melrede, held by Hardinius, besides two hides and three virgates in the hands of the Abbot. Two and a half hides in Melleburne. Half a virgate in Esceprid. Three hides, one virgate, and twelve acres in Harduic, besides ten acres detached. The Manor of Gratesdene, consisting of five hides. The Manor of Wivelingham, consisting of seven hides, and fifteen acres in Hochinton. The Manor of Epinstone, consisting of six hides and a half. The Manor of Coteham, consisting of ten hides. One hide and three virgates in Histone. The Manor of Whitesie, comprising two hides. Five hides and the Manor of Dodinton. Two hides and half a virgate in Cetriz. The Manor of Littleport, consisting of two and a half hides. One and a half hide in Stuntanei. One hide in Liteltedford. The Manor of Stradham, consisting of five hides. Five hides in Wimbertone. The Manor of Lindone, comprising nine hides. Two hides in Helle. Three hides in Hadreham. The Manor, consisting of ten hides, in Wisbece, with two fisheries. The Manor of Ely, consisting of ten hides. Four hides, including the Manor of Dineham. Three hides, with the Manor of Wiceford. Three and a half hides, including the Manor of Winteworde. Four hides and one virgate with Wiceham. The Manor of Sudstone, consisting of five hides. In *Huntingdonshire* : the Manor of Colne, consisting of six hides. Six and a half hides in Bluntesham. Eight hides, including the Manor of Sumersham. The Manor, and fifteen hides, at Shaldvice, with four hides forming the Manor of Parva Catenworde. And in *Essex*, the Manor of Brocheheshevot, comprising three hides. Three hides in Rodinges. The Manor of Ratenduna, comprising twenty hides. Two hides and the Manor of Cadenhoy. The Manor and twenty-five hides at Litelbyria, with half a hide and fifteen acres in the berewick of Hamdena.*

"A goodly array, I think you will agree with me, of the possessions belonging to the Church of Ely."

John Bull: "You have indeed given us evidence enough, I think, and to my mind overwhelming. I had no idea that you could bring forward such

* See Dugdale's 'Monasticum Anglicanum.' Ed. Galey, Ellis, Badinell. Vol. I., p. 461.

an array of proofs in support of the Church's title to property, and to so large an extent."

The Lady from Threadneedle Street : " Yes : the Church was rich in possessions in olden times; and there were men in days gone bye of large hearts and devoted lives; men and women who gave as largely and as freely in their day, as some of our best givers in these days, and as voluntarily offered their gifts to the service of God and His Church as any now do."

Mother Church : " What you say is indeed true, and it is a matter to rejoice in, even though the Church, since those days, has been grievously robbed of much of her property; for it is quite evident, from the various sources of information which we possess, that by the time of the Conquest and before the Pope got so much power and influence in this country, as he afterwards did,*

---

* 'Dean Hook says. " There are few instances of Papal power, in England, before the Norman Conquest. But the Pope having favoured and supported William I. in his invasion of this kingdom, made that a handle for enlarging his encroachments; and, in that King's reign began to send legates hither." Hook's Church Dictionary, p. 741. 5th Edition.

Hume also, speaking of the " Ecclesiastical administration" in England, at the time of the Conquest, says, "It had hitherto proved inaccessible to those exorbitant claims which supported the grandeur of the Papacy." History of England, I. p. 192.

And Blackstone, who is generally accurate as to his historical that the Church of England was very largely endowed. This is broadly asserted too by William the Conqueror, in a letter which he wrote to the Pope when he found he began to abuse the power William had permitted him to exercise, a copy of which letter is still to be found in a book printed in Latin, and afterwards published in English, at the time of the Reformation by Royal authority.* In this letter, which I claim *to put in as evidence also*, the Conqueror

data, says, "The Ancient British Church, by whomsoever planted, was a stranger to the Bishop of Rome, and all his pretended authority. But the pagan Saxon invaders having driven the professors of Christianity to the remotest corners of our island, their own conversion was afterwards effected by Augustine the Monk, and other missionaries from the Court of Rome. This naturally introduced some few of the papal corruptions in point of faith and doctrine; but we read of no civil authority claimed by the Pope in these kingdoms till the era of the Norman conquest, when the then reigning Pontiff having favoured Duke William in his projected invasion, by blessing his host and consecrating his banners, he took that opportunity also of establishing his spiritual encroachments; and was even permitted to do so by the policy of the Conqueror, in order more effectually to humble the Saxon clergy and aggrandize his Norman prelates; prelates, who, being bred abroad in the doctrine and practice of slavery, had contracted a reverence and regard for it, and took a pleasure in rivetting the chains of a free-born people." Com: on the Laws of Eng. IV. p. 95.

* See 'De vera Differentia inter Regium Potestatem et Ecclesiasticum,' fol. 89, A.D. 1547, a copy of which is to be found in the Library of the British Museum, 697.

says, 'The Church of England our Mother, which "among all Churches of the world doth excel and "abound in temporal possessions, and in the ser-"vice and honour of God, and in the diligence of "devout Ministers thereof, &c.' And then complaining that a number of foreign Clergymen had, through intrigue, got possession of many of her livings, and who cared only for the revenues and not for the flock they ought to have tended, William I. states that he will, by the help of God, protect the Church from such aliens, and goes on to say, '.Was this the first intent and "will and liberal mind of the Founders and Princes, "that the Alms and Patrimonies of Kings and "others which were assigned and given to the "Ministers of the Church for the exercise of the "honor of God and works of charity, should come "and remain to the profit of Aliens and Strangers? "Is this pleasing to God, that the Church so en-"dowed with possessions, which bringeth forth so "many discreet and wise children, profitable and "necessary to take cure and ministration of here, "should let her own Children be in hunger and "penury, to give her paps to Aliens and Strangers, "not only to take suck of them, but rather to tear "and pull them to pieces; for the children suck

"the milk, strangers wring out the blood, letting
"nothing remain that they may snatch and pluck,"
etc.

"These words of the Conqueror seem to tally fully with the evidence I have already adduced from other sources; he acknowledges that the Church of England in his day abounded in temporal possessions; and that they were derived from the alms and gifts of pious Founders and Princes, without one word to intimate that the endowments of the Church arose from any national grant. And it may interest you, if, in conclusion, I produce before you a translation or complete copy which has been preserved, of *a deed of gift*, by one of our ancient Princes, as it is just what our opponents have asked for, and will shew that our kings and princes gave alms and lands from what belonged to them, and which they inherited from their ancestors, and not what belonged to the nation."

The charter of Edward the Confessor, granting lands to Westminster Abbey.

"Edward King, greeteth Wlsy, Bishop, and
"Gyrth, Earl, and all my nobles in Oxfordshire.
"And I tell you that I have given to Christ and
"St. Peter in Westminster that small village

"wherein I was born, by name Githslepe,* and
"one hide at Mersee, scot-free and rent-free,
"with all the things belonging thereunto in wood
"and field, in meadows and waters, with Church
"and the immunities of the Church as fully, and
"as largely, and as free, as it stood in mine own
"hand, and also as my mother *Imme* upon my
"right of primogeniture, for my maintenance,
"gave it me entire, and bequeathed it to the
"family."†

And now, in bringing my proofs of title to property to a close, I would would make two or three remarks. First, it is evident, from the various instances that have come to our notice, that many of our Parish Churches are anciently indebted to these Monasteries for their endowments, though it is likely that the larger number were founded by private munificence. The Clergy that went forth from these Monasteries, however, into the country and villages round about, preaching the Gospel, would often settle down among the people to whom they became attached; or some other Clergyman would

* Called elsewhere 'Gibtslepe,' and, by dropping a Saxon letter or two became *Islip*; just as *Gipewic* became *Ipswich*, and *Gifteley*, *Ifley*, near Oxford.

† M.S. Numb. 24, James in Musœo, Bid. Bod., p. 51.

be permanently appointed, and then the Monastery would apportion him and his successors a regular income from their lands or funds, especially if they held lands in the place; keeping, with the approval of the Bishop of the Diocese, the future appointment of Clergymen in their own hands."

"Again, our evidence shews us that it is a great mistake, a mere vulgar error, for people to think that the Church of England is indebted to the Church of Rome, to any large extent, for her endowments previous to the Reformation. These endowments of the Church of England were mainly and chiefly given before the Popes of Rome gained that usurped authority over the Church in this country, which they did acquire between the times of the Conquest and the Reformation. The Church of Rome has, I assert, taken far more from the Church of England than she ever gave. The Church of Rome has been too often as an incubus, or blood-sucker, to the Church of England, oppressing her and diminishing her strength. However much or however little was gained to the Church of England during the time the Church of Rome held the sway over her, that amount, and much more that really belonged to the Church of England before the

L

Conquest, was afterwards taken away from her, by, and through, the connivance of the State; for the fact must be patent to all students of our English history, that the Church of England was much poorer *after* she was delivered from the domination of the Church of Rome, than she was before she came under that domination, as the evidence of the times of the Conquest and after the Reformation fully proves."

"And once more. It will be observed that, in the evidence I have brought before you, I have not dealt with Episcopal and Cathedral endowments; time will not allow us to do this: I would, however, observe that it is not true to state as an 'historical fact,' as it has been stated, that these establishments of the Church were founded *after* the Conquest. Many of the Cathedrals were rebuilt after the Conquest, but they were founded, and the main bulk of the endowments for maintaining them were given and acquired *before* the Conquest; and in support of this statement I would simply draw your attention to the account which Dugdale, in his Monasticum (p. 273), gives us respecting the dates when the following Cathedrals in the Church of England were founded.

	A.D.		A.D.
Canterbury	600	Wells	676
Gloucester	189	Lichfield	666
Rochester	600	Exeter	990
Winchester	639	Landaff	180
Worcester	683	St. Asaph	560
Chester	660	Durham	635
York	625	Oxford	727
St. David's	530	Peterborough	656
London	610	Ely	673

"It may therefore be taken for granted that the *Endowments* for *our Cathedrals*, and the support for their several staff of officers, as well as the *Episcopal Endowments* were originally provided by the voluntary gifts of earnest and devoted Churchmen in days long ago : for this also could be proved, did time permit, in a similar manner to what has been done in regard to *Minsters* or the ancient monasteries, which were so useful to the Church of England before they got into papal hands."

"And as regards the *Re-building of some of our Cathedrals* during the period when the Church of England was subjected to the Pope, we must remember that they were rebuilt with *English* money, and not with any money which came from the Church of Rome. The money for re-building them was raised chiefly from property belonging to the ancient foundations, and from the alms and gifts of pious English Churchmen. The Church of England was no gainer by the domination of the Church of Rome, and certainly the Church of Rome has no claim, or moral right, to any of our ecclesiastical buildings; to some of the Monasteries founded before the Reformation, but which were then taken away by the State, it might have some claim, but not to our Cathedrals, and Minsters, and Abbeys."

John Bull: "I am glad you make this appear plain, because in the minds of many there is a confused notion that the Roman Catholics had some claim, or partly so, to them, and that it was only national prejudice that denied them any title to them."

Mother Church: "I have no doubt the Romanists in this country endeavour to foster such an idea. It is but a popular error, however, to suppose that we are indebted for the money or means whereby we erected our venerable Cathedrals and Minsters to the Church of Rome. Not only did the Church of Rome, proper, not contribute to the building of them, but she took away very much money from the Church of England, to erect and maintain her own Churches;* so that, if a righteous balance were made between the two, it would be found that the Church of Rome was much in debt to the Church of England, and that the Church of Rome had no moral or just claim to any of the property which the Church of England now possesses."

* At one time the Church of Rome fairly fleeced us. In the reign of Henry III. the exactions from the Church of England were something enormous. Hear what Hume says, whose statements are corroborated by other authorities. "Pope Honorious, in 1226, complaining of the poverty of the see (of Rome) as the source of all grievances, demanded from every Cathedral two of the best prebends, and from every Convent two monks' portions, to be set apart as a perpetual and settled revenue of the Papal Crown. . . . About three years after, the Pope demanded and obtained the tenth of all ecclesiastical revenues, which he levied in a very oppressive manner; requiring payment before the Clergy had drawn their rents or tithes, and sending about usurers who advanced them money at exorbitant interest. In the year 1240, Otho the legate, having in vain attempted the Clergy in a body, obtained separately, by intrigues and menaces, large sums from the prelates and convents, and on his departure is said to have carried more money out of the kingdom than he left iu it. This experiment was renewed four years after with success by Martin the Nuncio, who brought from Rome powers of suspending and excommunicating all clergymen who refused to comply with his demands. The king, who relied on the pope for the support of his tottering authority, never failed to countenance those exactions.

"Meanwhile, all the chief benefices of the kingdom were conferred on Italians: great numbers of that nation were sent over at one time to be provided for; non-residence and pluralities were carried to an enormous height."—History of England, vol. II, p. 159.

"And now I have finished, for the present, what I have to say respecting the Landed endowments, as also the Buildings, of the Church, and must leave the matter in your hands."

Madame Britannia: "Thank you, very much. And in concluding our Conference to day, I would take the privilege of saying to you, venerable Lady, (addressing Mother Church), that you have right nobly taken up the challenge thrown down by your adversaries,—you have thoroughly contested the statements of those opposed to you, and to my mind you have fully vindicated the Right of the Church to the possession and use of her endowments. I have little doubt but that the verdict of the country will be decidedly in your favour, when this cause becomes known to them. And I think from the approving nods which our friend here, Mr. Bull, has given, he agrees with what I have said."

John Bull: "Yes, I do Madam; for I was never more thoroughly convinced of anything in all my life than I am now, of the Right of the Church to her property; and, from the proofs which have been given, that she has a valid title to it also."

Mother Church here intimated that she had most of her evidence ready as regarded *the Tithes* belonging to the Church, as well as other points of evidence to support what has been advanced respecting the Church's voluntarily endowments, especially those which are *Parochial*, the which she must now defer giving till a future occasion; and she begged as a favour that the time of their next meeting together might be deferred to a later period of the year, for, as she stated, she had many things of importance to attend to, and some of which could not be well delayed.

They all agreed to this, and thought it would be better, and more convenient also to themselves. They then bid adieu to each other, and parted.

PART V.

After an interval of a few months, the Three Venerable Ladies again met together by appointment, Mr. Bull also being present, as on former occasions. After the usual greetings and expressions of goodwill and kindly feeling had been made,

Madam Britannia opened the way for discussion by saying, "I think the subject for our consideration to-day is, *the Right which the Church has to the Endowment of Tithes;* and, if I remember rightly, our venerable friend, Mother Church, promised to lay before us some clear statement as to the origin of Tithes, and on what grounds the Church possesses a lawful right to them."

John Bull: "I shall gladly sit and listen to the discussion on this subject, as there appears to be a great many difficulties and objections raised about it which has a tendency to confuse men's minds, and to perplex them, so that they are unable to decide for themselves quite clearly as to the matter. I shall be right well pleased, therefore, to hear the plain truth about Tithes from those who have studied the subject, in the face of these difficulties and objections."

The Lady from Threadneedle Street: "It is true that some doubt and uncertainty has of late been thrown over the right which the Church has to this kind of property; but this, we must remember, arises from those who are enemies to the Church, and who purposely design to deprive the Church of her lawful property in this respect, and therefore, begin their attack by bringing forwards and heaping up all manner of objections. But I charge them, as in other matters, so in this, with a suppression of the truth,—with gross misrepresentations of the subject,—and with purposely twisting statements and facts to effect their design. And I contend, that if this can be clearly proved against them, then, as in the case of witnesses in a court of justice, their statements and evidences must fall to the ground and be set aside.

"I stand by the side of my venerable friend to assist her in her defence of her rights, and if I may be permitted, I will give you an illustration or proof of what I have advanced from the words of one of the leaders of this attack against the Church, and the manner in which a false colouring is given to the subject in various points, and where matters have been kept back which would have helped to substantiate the Church's right to Tithes. For during our recess, I have taken some pains to look into the matter. Mr. Miall, in his book called 'The Title-Deeds of the Church,' states that 'the Christian Church knew nothing of Tithes for above 400 years after the Ascension of her Lord to the throne of His spiritual kingdom,'* and then he gives a reference to Selden in support of what he says. But Selden's words are somewhat different to his, and he omits to say what Selden says on this point in a review of his book at the end, which Selden implores his readers to take up and read with the former part; and we there find him saying, 'I was not so bold as to make the negative *that no Tithes* were paid, but that it could not be proved that any were.' 'He that can show me ought omitted that might prove it, shall deserve and have thanks of me.'† But what Selden dare not say, Mr. Miall dare, though

* Chap. II. p. 6.
† Selden on Tithes, p. 460, 461.

he has chiefly to depend for his facts upon Selden;* and, moreover, Mr. Miall keeps back part of the truth, which is stated by Selden, for he does not tell us that Selden would not speak positively, or, at least, that he spoke hesitatingly or doubtfully upon the points, as if it were possible that evidence might be forthcoming to show that Tithes *were paid* during the first 400 years. Then, again, Selden says, in the beginning of his 5th chapter, 'About the beginning of the next (400 years), or rather some years before the end of the first part of this division, and afterwards, *Tenths were paid*, or for holy uses offered (as the phrase was) in divers places, in offerings of that quantity; and some testimony is of *Churches also endowed with the perpetual right* of them in the latter half of this four hundred years. Great opinion *was now of their*

---

* Mr. Miall had been taunted, that nearly all the learning which he exhibited was second-hand, and chiefly borrowed from Selden's work; and, in his 2nd edition, 1871, he appears to be very angry at the remarks made by his critics, but is compelled to allow the truth of what is stated, for he says: "The reply is easy. But for the aid offered by Selden, it is probable that I should not have undertaken my task, or, rather, not have dealt with the subject in precisely the manner I did. I joyfully and openly accepted the results of the immense and unequalled learning of that author."

being due.'* But let us go back to the very words which Mr. Miall mistakes and misrepresents. The heading of the 4th chapter in Selden begins thus : ' No use of Tithes occurs *till* about the end of this [first] four hundred years.' And after a few introductory words, Selden says, ' Till towards the end of the first four hundred years no payment of them can be proved to have been in use. Some opinion is of their being due.'* Surely these words mean that, towards the end of the first four hundred years, *some proofs might be adduced of payment of Tithes,* not, as Mr. Miall has it, that Christians knew nothing of Tithes for above 400 years after the Ascension — that is, till about A.D. 430. Mr. Miall, therefore, in this point, says the very opposite thing to Selden, who is his authority for what he states. Then Mr. Miall keeps back the reason, which Mr. Selden gives, why we must not expect to meet with proofs of Tithes, as such, being paid earlier. ' For the first,' says Selden, ''tis best declared by showing the course of the Church maintenance in that time. So liberal, in the beginning of Christianity, was the devotion of Believers, that their bounty to the Evangelical priest-

* Selden, p. 46.   † Ibid, p. 35

hood *far exceeded what the tenth could have been.*
For, if you look to the first of the Apostles' times,
then the unity of heart among them about Jerusalem was such that all was in common, and none
wanted, and 'As many as were possessors of lands
or houses sold them, and brought the price of the
things that were sold and laid them at the Apostles'
feet, and it was distributed to every man as he had
need.' And the whole Church, both lay and
clergy, then lived in common as the monks did
afterwards about the end of the first 400 years, as
St. Chrysostom notes.'* And, again, in his Review
at the end, Selden says, ' But it has been little to
the purpose, indeed, to have had Tithes of annual
increase paid, while that most bountiful devotion
of good Christians continued in frequent offerings,
both of lands and goods to such large value. Also,
questionless, the liberal devotion of the time was
very exceeding in offerings.'† Can it be honest in
Mr. Miall, I ask, or is he giving a fair representation, think you, of the subject, when he keeps such
a reason out of sight, when it stands directly in his
way in Selden's book ? Why he omits it is but too

* " So they live now in monasteries, as then the Believers'
lived."—Homil. Acts II. v. 44.
† Selden, p. 562.

obvious,—it militates against his argument, and supports that of the Church."

Mother Church: "I may, perhaps, here at this point be allowed to say respecting Selden, that, though a Puritan, he was a man of undoubted learning and great research, as well as one of the ablest lawyers of his time. But those who read his book will notice that he is continually trying to throw discredit on ancient testimony, and set it aside as valueless. Of course it is always difficult to vouch for statements in those remote times, still there is much that we may credit; and Mr. Selden seems to have gone to the opposite extreme; nevertheless, there is this to be urged, that what he does state, and passes as worthy of credit, on such a subject, may be the more safely credited, as having passed through a searching ordeal. I would only make this other remark, that when Selden wrote this book of Tithes, he was not yet 33 years old; and that other authors having taken the subject up, showing where he had erred, and given a wrong view of the points he had touched, he, in after years, is fain to confess that he had made some mistakes. I name this because, though there is much that we can approve of in Selden's work, there are some points in which we cannot hold with him.* I hope my kind friend will pardon this interruption, but I thought it better to make these remarks before proceeding further."

The Lady from Threadneedle Street: "I thank you, for the remarks come seasonably, and are needed. But to proceed with my allegations. Mr. Miall says: 'The public laws of England, and not the private liberality of individuals, created the Tithe system, as a provision for the maintenance of the clergy of this country.'† But surely the clergy were maintained before any public laws were made about Tithes, and how, but by the pri-

---

* Dean Comber says of Selden that, "forgetting his fair professions (see his preface), he conceals some of the best proofs for Tithes, rejects others, and questions all that seem to establish the Divine Right or universal practice of Tithes, greedily searching after, and plausibly setting off, all that appear to make against it. Yet I am confident divers have stretched some passages of this book further than ever Mr. S. intended, and have drawn conclusions which he (if yet alive) would blush to see."—Preface to Comber on Tithes.

Selden is also severely handled by Montagne, afterwards Bishop of Winchester, in his "Diatribæ." Dr. Tilesly also, in another work, convicts Selden of many errors. Those who study Selden, and are curious to note his errors, will find a number of them pointed out and controverted in Collier's Ecclesiastical History, Book vii., p. 39.

† Miall's Title-Deeds of the Church of England, p. 26.

vate liberality of individuals; and Selden expressly admits that, some hundreds of years before the English laws were made, Tithes were paid and considered to be due, pp. 35, 46. This you must perceive is the very opposite of Mr. Miall's assertion, and cuts the ground from under his feet. And, it was because Tithes were considered to be due to the Church, as the common law of the realm—the *jus commune* or *folk-right*—that one charter after another was made to protect the right of the Church in this matter, so that those who cared not for religion, might not escape payment, as they so often tried to do. But as you, my venerable friend, (turning to Mother Church) have already made some suitable observations on this point,' (See pp. 91-93,) I will pass on to another.

"Alluding to an Act of Parliament passed in Edward VI.'s reign (2 and 3, ch. 13, sec. 5), Mr. Miall, after making various calculations as to what land was formerly under cultivation, in comparison of what is now cultivated, says, '*there remains*, therefore, only *one-fourth of the Tithe property now existing* which could by any possibility have grown out of lay liberality.'* Well, this is certainly an

* Miall's Title-Deeds, p. 56.

important admission, after he started out with the positive assertion, which he puts in italics at the beginning of his book, 'that they (Tithes) neither did, nor in the nature of things could, originate in private individual liberality.'* But to admit what he has done destroys the truthfulness of this grand assertion of his with which he sets out, or, at least, shows that he has made a very reckless and unwarrantable statement. The truth evidently appears to be this: Mr. Miall had been looking somewhat more closely into the question, in order to support the position he had taken up—he has made great search into Selden, and he is now somewhat shaken in his mind about the truth of what he had stated at the beginning, and thinks it even possible that one fourth might possibly *have grown* out of lay liberality.'

"But now see what he says further with respect to the results of the Act in Edward VI.'s reign. He goes on to say, 'The other three-fourths are directly traceable, not to private grants, not even to custom or common law, but to the legislation of Parliament. Three fourths of the parochial endowments of the Church of England [consisting of

* Ibid, p. 5.

Tithes],* have their root in an Act of Parliament passed a little more than three hundred years ago. Let that fact be explained away, if it can be, by those who contend for the sacredness and inalienability of Tithe endowments, on the ground of their being consecrated by individual piety.'†

"Now, how is this grave statement of Mr. Miall's to be met ? I reply, By simply denying its truth ; there is no ground for the assertion he makes ; he has made a serious mistake, and it arises from his not reading or understanding the Act aright, for I will not in this point accuse him of a wilful design to misrepresent the matter ; I accuse him here not of knowingly perverting the truth, but of obtuseness of comprehension. The Act was made really for the benefit of the Farmer, who made improvements, and not for the benefit of the Tithe-owner ; for the latter was restrained for seven years from getting more Tithes than he had formerly done on reclaimed lands, or lands

* These words had been omitted in the former edition, but introduced into the 2nd edition, 1871, for it had been pointed out to him that his words were altogether inapplicable to the other endowments of the Church. Indeed, he frequently in his 1st edition makes a jumble of other endowments with that of Tithes, which has led many that follow him into gross errors.

† Miall's Title-Deeds, pp. 57, 57.

otherwise improved. But let me give you the words of a certain barrister-at-law, who has carefully examined this point. He says: 'To contradict the statement and to prove its absurdity is not difficult. Three-fourths of the endowments of the parochial incumbents of the Church of England had not their root in this Act of Parliament.'*
Then, Mr. Pulman, goes on to show how the Act is to be read, and that Mr. Miall's statement is not borne out by the Act, and concludes by saying, 'that this Act of Parliament 'called Tithes into existence,' *is not a fact, nor is it law.*' This is plain, for by it Tithes have only to be paid on lands which were titheable beforehand; but, in order to encourage farmers and owners of property to bring their land into cultivation, they were not to be charged any more Tithes, for seven years, than they had hitherto paid, so that farmers might reap for that period the advantage of their toil; the Act, in short, did what a wise landlord might do, who would say to his tenant, 'if you choose to bring those lands which yield little or nothing into cultivation, you shall not pay me more for them than what you have formerly done for seven years, but after that period

* Pulman's Anti-State Church, &c., Unmasked, p. 126.

you must pay me the proper and marketable rent for them.' A special exception is made in the Act for lands not titheable before this. The words of the Act are as follows; and, by carefully reading it over, you will soon see the gross error into which Mr. Miall has fallen. Section 4th, which Mr. Miall omits :

'No person shall be sued or otherwise compelled to yield, give or pay any manner of Tithes for any Manor, Lands, Tenements, or Hereditaments, which by the Laws and Statutes of this Realm, or by any privilege or prescription are not chargeable with the payment of such Tithes, or be discharged by any composition real.'

This is in itself a sufficient reply to Mr. Miall's assertion. Section 5, which he does quote, and which should be read after what goes before, is as follows :

' That all such barren heath and waste ground, *other than such as be discharged for the payment of Tithes* by Act of Parliament, which before this time have lain barren, and *paid no Tithe by reason of the same barrenness*, and now be, or hereafter shall be improved and converted into arable ground or meadow, shall from henceforth after the end and term of seven years next after such improvement fully ended and determined, pay Tithe for the corn and hay growing on the same.*

"Read together, we see that this payment of Tithes after seven years applies *only* to lands already chargeable with Tithe, but had not paid Tithe by reason of barrenness. This view is further proved by what follows in Section 6, which Mr. Miall also omits, which relates to cases where a small amount had formerly been paid for waste or barren land, and in such cases the amount shall not be *increased* till after the seven years.

"Moreover, Mr. Miall's calculations of three-fourths are notoriously wrong, inasmuch as they are founded upon the supposition that the clergy receive the Tithes, or a composition for them, *upon all lands now under cultivation*, which is not true; for there are many lands brought into cultivation up and down the country, which have been exempt from paying Tithe.

"Mr. Miall has also been very unfortunate in fixing upon the period of Edward VI.'s reign as a time when he imagines an Act of Parliament was passed which 'called Tithes into existence,' for it

* 2 and 3 Ed. VI., chap. 13, A.D. 1548.

was notoriously a time when Parliament suffered the Church to be filched and robbed to an enormous extent, so as to impoverish her to such a degree that she was not able to cope with the religious requirements of the period, and in consequence of which the people began to support ministers of their own, which brought in much religious dissension and even persecution. And this period, in which Mr. Miall has so unfortunately chosen to imagine such an accession of Tithe property coming to the Church, is the one, which his favourite author, Selden, especially marks out as being that, in which the property of the Church was so woefully laid waste by the secular arm.

* After alluding to "the prodigal dispensation . . . on those who stood ready to devour that which was sanctified," Selden adds, "But I abstain from censure, and add here by the way a complaint made to the Parliament, not long after the dissolution, touching the abuse that followed in the Church through laymen's possessing of Appropriated Churches and Tithes. It deserves to be seriously thought on, continues Selden, by every layman that now enjoys any of them, especially where Divine service is not carefully provided for. Addressing 'the Lords and Burgesses of Parliament,' the complaint commences, 'I require of you, in the name of my poor brethren that are Englishmen and members of Christ's Body, that ye consider well (as ye will answer before the face of Almighty God, in the Day of Judgment) this abuse, and see it amended.' Further on, the complaint says, 'Your pretence of putting down Abbeys, was to amend that was amiss in them.

If, then, Mr. Miall had not been so grievously blinded by his malevolent assault on the Church, it would certainly have been impressed upon his mind that this was not a likely time for Parliament to make an Act, whereby the Church should acquire such a large increase of Tithes.

"I will not adduce other instances of errors,

. . . But see now how it that was amiss is amended, for all the godly pretence. It is amended even as the Devil amended his Dame's leg (as it is in the Proverb), when he should have set it right, he brake it quite to pieces. The monks gave too little alms, and set unable persons many times in their benofices. But now where xx. pound was given yearly to the poor, in more than a hundred places in England is not one meals' meat given. This is a 'feare' amendment. Where they had always one or other vicar, that either preached, or hired some to preach, now is there no vicar at all; but the farmer is vicar and parson altogether, and only an old cast-away friar or monk, which can scarce say his mattins, is hired for twenty or thirty shillings, meat and drink, yea, in some places for meat and drink alone, without any wages. I know, and not I alone, but twenty thousand more, know more than 500 vicarages and parsonages thus well and Gospelly served, after the new Gospel of England.' And then Selden adds, 'And so the Author goes on with sharp admonitions to laymen, tha fed themselves fat with the Tithes of such Churches, while the souls of the Parishioners suffered great famino for want of a fit pastor, that is, for want of fit maintenance for him, for without that, he is scarce to be hoped for.' Did Mr. Miall never see these words? And why is it that whilst Selden so severely condemns this confiscation of Tithe property, Mr Miall is so anxious that Parliament should again consent to despoil the Church of it!"

though many others are to be found, as noted by Mr. Pulman, who states that Selden, Burns, Acts of Parliament in other places, Macaulay, and other authors referred to by Mr. Miall, are uniformly misrepresented in their statements."*

John Bull : " Well ; no wonder people are perplexed and in some uncertainty about the question of Tithes, when such a pack of errors, as we have here, are foisted on them. It is like throwing dust into people's eyes to prevent their having a notion of what is the right view to take of them. And I suppose that all those who look upon Mr. Miall as a kind of leader against the Church, take all that he says 'for Gospel.' Its just, to my mind, a case of the ' blind leaders of the blind.'"

The Old Lady from Threadneedle Street : " Yes, this is the worst of it : and the evil grows, and gathers strength, to a marvellous degree : for, as it appears, from the little work by a Baptist minister, entitled ' Church Property : what is it, and whose ?' and from the letters of some Dissenting preachers, which I have seen, and to which you have already alluded, Mr. Bull,—there are many political Dissenting preachers who not only repeat many of Mr. Miall's errors, but often magnify

* Pulman, p. 34.

them, and doubtless frequently retail them out to their hearers, till they believe in them; the one is too ready to give utterance, and the other too ready to believe any kind of tale, if it be only against the Church: and thus a powerful section of the community is ever embittered against the Church, and led to join in this unchristian crusade against her."

Madam Britannia: "This is a sad state of things; and one much to be lamented, for there is little prospect of peace or satisfaction to be expected so long as these people are so wofully misled. I think, however, Madam, that you have discharged a most important duty in your endeavour to expose these errors, as it will help to take the veil off men's eyes, and the better enable them to see the true state of the case, and to judge for themselves."

John Bull: "Yes, Madam, that is what is wanted. We want to know the truth! For the people of England are, at the bottom, sound and honest, and like to see justice done; and will resolutely stand up for it too, let them but be truly incensed with the right of it."

Madam Britannia: "And now, if it be agreeable to you all, I should like to hear what our venerable friend, Mother Church, has to say upon the subject."

Mother Church : " The time has been well spent hitherto, I consider ; and I must again thank my worthy friend for the service she has done me in the cause which I have in hand. Some points of history to which I may allude may be known to you already, but forasmuch as the subject has been so much questioned that many persons have got but a hazy notion of the truth of the matter, I shall endeavour to set it before you in some order, to the best of my ability.

" It is a settled point, which our opponents admit, and which we are willing to take for granted, that *the first civil enactment, for the whole of England, to obtain the regular and perpetual payment of Tithes*, was the Charter, granted by King Ethelwulf about the year 855. We have, however, the account of a civil enactment to enforce the payment of Tithes, as due, for large portions of the island before this, *i.e.*, during the Heptarchy; but it could not well be made for the whole island much sooner than the time I have named, because, as it is well known to the readers of History, that England did not become a united kingdom until the year 827, when Egbert, the first king, brought the Heptarchy to an end. He was sometime, as might be expected, in consolidating his new kingdom as a whole. Ethelwulf was his son and successor; and it was by the advice and consent of the great men of his kingdom, assembled in Council, that this Charter, to which we have alluded to, was given.

"I need not trouble you with the whole of the Charter, but the portion which we are most concerned to know runs thus, when translated :—

'I, Ethelwulf, by the grace of God, King of the West Saxons, with the advice of the Bishops, Earls, and all the persons of condition in my dominions, have for the health of my soul, the good of my people, and the prosperity of my kingdom, fixed upon a prudent and serviceable resolution of granting the tenth part of the lands throughout our kingdom to the Holy Churches and ministers of religion, officiating, and settled in them, with all the advantages of a free tenure and estate.'*

"There is a second Charter by the same king, recorded by Ingulph, the old Saxon chronicler, in which allusion is made to the ravages of war, and the depredations of enemies, as the occasion or

* Vide Collier's Eccles. Hist., Book iii., p. 368.

necessity which led him to resolve upon a wholesome and uniform remedy.*

"Now before we proceed to trace the history of Tithes further up the stream of time, or trace it downwards from this period, it is desirable—whilst on this acknowledged standing-ground,—to consider what is the weight and significance of this grant of Tithes to the Church, and the circumstances attending it.

"And the first consideration we should notice is this, that Tithes had been paid, and generally considered due as a right, before this. It was one great means of maintenance to the clergy long before Ethelwulf's time, and it was not now for the first time they enjoyed them. Many owners of property (it was then in fewer hands than it is now) recognised their obligation to religion in this respect, and made their lands chargeable with Tithes, and not only paid Tithes themselves as owing to the Church, but handed down their property to their successors with this charge upon it.

* The other Charter is dated the year before, *i.e.*, A.D. 854. And Collier is of opinion, from its wording, that the first related to the "Tithes of the king's demesnes or crown lands." And that the one the year after, "made by the consent of the nobility and people, enlarged the bounty, and extended it to the whole kingdom," p. 363.

As the people became Christians, property was generally received on the understanding that a tenth portion could be claimed by the Church: for the ancient Saxons called it 'God's right,' God's fee;' and the laws of King Withred forbid laymen possessing things anciently given to God, A.D. 694. And, again, A.D. 697, he enjoined that 'the Church should have its revenues.'* The practice or custom must therefore have been in existence some time before this. But more of this presently. There were, however, some, as you may imagine, who cared not for religion, who regarded the paying of Tithes as so much of their own which they had to give up, and would try to avoid paying them, and regarded it as a matter in which they could please themselves: and as there was then no law to compel the payment of Tithes, or only such as had fallen into abeyance, the Church was frequently robbed of her lawful maintenance; and it was necessary that the ruling powers in the land, and those who had authority to decree and uphold what was right in the country, should recognise the Church's right in this respect, and make it distinctly understood

* Spel. Concil. Tom i., pp. 189 and 194.

that in every part of the country they must be paid, as lawfully due to the Church : hence the Charter of Ethelwulf.

"Hume, the great historian of English history, has made some sarcastic remarks upon the granting of this Charter, which has been quoted and put forward by our opponents, but from which we may gather some truth. He says :

'The ecclesiastics, in those days of ignorance, . . . not content with the donations of land made them by the princes and nobles, and with temporary oblations from the devotions of the people, had cast a wistful eye upon a vast revenue, which they claimed as belonging to them by a sacred and indefeasible title. . . . During some centuries the whole scope of sermons and homilies was directed to this purpose ; and one would have imagined, from the general tenour of these discourses, that all the practical parts of Christianity were comprised in the exact and faithful payment of tithes to the clergy. . .
Though parishes had been instituted in England by Honorious, Archbishop of Canterbury, near two centuries before, the ecclesiastics had never been able to get possession of the Tithes; they therefore seized the present favourable opportunity

of making that acquisition when a weak, superstitious prince filled the throne, &c.'*

"Now it must be borne in mind that Hume was a Deist, and could not view religion, of any sort, with favour: with him all religion was folly, and repentance was weakness. Supposing Ethelwulf had been a weak prince—and perhaps he was in comparison with his father;—yet this could not be the case with 'the Bishops, *Earls, and all the persons of condition in his dominion.*' Could they all be weak? There was surely strength of mind and will amongst these men to have resisted any unreasonable attempt to impose upon them any unjust or mere superstitious grant, if they had conceived this grant of Ethelwulf's to have been such. But as they did not, and as it appeared, on the contrary, that *this grant was made by their advice*, it is quite evident they considered it to be a proper, just, and reasonable thing to be done.

"The expression used in Ethelwulf's Charter, viz., his '*granting* the tenth part of the land,' does not imply that the clergy had not a right to the Tithes before this, or that this was the original grant of them; but that Ethelwulf herein, as the *sovereign of the land*, granted the Church *a legal*

* Hume's Hist. Eng., vol. i., pp. 84, 85.

title to the Tithes, so that the clergy might enforce their claim to them by law, and call in the authority of the civil power to compel the payment of them whenever the Tithes were withheld; for hitherto in many cases they had been unable to recover them from those who had little regard for religion, although these persons, on coming into possession of their several properties, knew that the Tithes were due to the Church, as of right. The owners of the soil had a more prompt and direct means of redress. Should their tenants refuse them rent, service, or a fixed portion of their produce, they could seize upon what they considered equivalent, or turn the tenants off, or, being serfs, administer summary punishment for defalcation; but the tenth portion which belonged to the Church, by prescription, could not thus be recovered, and being often withheld, and the fraud connived at by covetous or ungodly landlords, the clergy were frequently deprived of their maintenance; it was therefore found necessary to make the payment legal and obligatory upon all, by the highest authority in the land, viz., by the king in a council of the realm. But this insuring the due payment of Tithes to the Church, through this grant of a legal Title, whereby the civil power assured the Church of its support in obtaining them regularly for the future, was a very different thing from making a gift of them, as of something that did not already belong to them; for, as I hope to show you still further, Tithes were given and received before this.

"Referring to the grant, 'we are to bear in mind,' says Dean Hook, 'that an Anglo-Saxon king was only the chieftain of the people, not the owner of the soil. Although he possessed certain rights and claimed certain dues, he was only one among the landed proprietors: Ethelwulf could not give what he did not possess,—he simply devoted to religious and charitable purposes a tenth part of his private estates, and released from all payments due to him as king a tenth part of the land unfranchised.'[*] Another well-known writer of Anglo-Saxon history states also respecting the grant of Ethelwulf that, 'It has been considered as the *legislative enactment* by which the lands were first subjected to the payment of Tithes to the clergy; but the right of the Church had already been recognised in the most unequivocal manner.' [†]

[*] Lives of the Archbishops of Canterbury, I. 287.
[†] Palgrave, I., 159.

"Moreover, we have this argument in favour of the Church's ancient right to Tithes to bring in here, that from the mention of the King acting 'by the advice of the Bishops, Earls, and all the persons of condition in his dominion,' it is evident that they were the principal owners of land in the kingdom, who were then present, and, that as such, they had a perfect right, as much as men of property have in these days, to make a grant of Tithes from their own lands, in perpetuity to the Church, by and through the King as their head and representative. Therefore, if even this occasion of making a grant by Charter had been indeed the first bestowal of Tithes, it would give the Church the best title and security for the enjoyment of the Tithes that could be given: how much more then does it serve to establish the right of the Church to this kind of endowment, when the Charter appears to have been, as it was, a confirmation of an acknowledged payment due to the Church, which had grown up among them, and had come to be looked upon generally as belonging to the Church from earlier days, though withheld by some who cared not for religion."

The Lady from Threadneedle Street: "Neither can it be said, as it has been hinted, that the grant was forced upon these great men, who were the chief possessors of land in the country, when it is confessedly acknowledged that Ethelwulf was 'a weak prince.' It is both indefensible and ridiculous to suppose that these sturdy Anglo-Saxons,— *Earls and all the persons of condition* in the king's dominion, would have suffered Ethelwulf, at the instigation of the clergy, to have wrested a tenth portion of the produce of their lands from them, even for pious purposes, unless they felt, as they undoubtedly did, that the Church had some right and claim to it. Such a thing could not be done then, any more than it could be done now. The very statement of the transaction itself is sufficient to prove that such an attempt would never have been made, and that the great council of the nation would never have consented to have a portion of their property severally taken from them at the arbitrary dictation of a Sovereign, who altogether depended upon them for support against his enemies who continually threatened him. No! the very expression, that this Charter granting the Tithes, was given '*by the advice* of the Earls and all the persons of condition,' shows that they readily consented to it, if they did not urge it upon the King, as a matter of right to be done to the

Church,—that he, as the representative of lawful authority, should make this grant for *securing, not creating*, the Tithes, already considered as belonging to the Church. According to Judge Blackstone, it was the grand and fundamental maxim of ancient English tenure, that all lands were granted out by the Sovereign, and that no change, transfer, or even mortgage could be made, or be counted valid, without leave or grant to do this from the Crown*; it was therefore as the Lord Paramount of the soil, that Ethelwulf made the grant, and it cannot be regarded as an act of despotism, whereby he made the owners of property pay Tithes, and accept as a perpetual charge upon their property the payment of Tithes, whether they liked it or not. Do not, however, let me further interrupt my friend in her statement."

Mother Church: "Thank you; you do not interrupt me, but rather supplement what I might have omitted; but to proceed. That Tithes belonged to, and were acknowledged as the right of the Church *before Ethelwulf's days*, also, we have further satisfactory evidence to produce. Judge Blackstone 'on the Laws of England' says, 'We cannot precisely ascertain the time when Tithes

* Blackstone's Com., Vol. ii., 54, 58, 60.

were first introduced into this country. Possible they were contemporary with the planting of Christianity among the Saxons by Augustine the monk, about the end of the sixth century. But the first mention of them, which I have met with *in any written English law*, is a constitutional decree, made in Synod, held A.D. 786, wherein the payment of Tithes is strongly enjoined. This canon or decree, which at first bound not the laity, was effectually confirmed by two kingdoms of the Heptarchy, respectively consisting of the Kings of Mercia and Northumberland, the Bishops, Dukes, Senators and people.'* The law of Offa, which is here referred to, is thus worded. 'Wherefore with obtestation we enjoin that all be careful to pay Tithes of all they possess, because they are the special property of the Lord our God; and maintain themselves, and give alms of the nine parts,'† *i.e.*, on the nine parts, which belong to them, they are to live and make voluntary offerings as they like, but the tenth part is not theirs, but belongs to the Church, and therefore payment of this is obligatory upon them. Selden remarks upon it, 'it is a most observable law to this purpose, being

* Blackstone, Com., Vol. ii., p. 28.
† Selden, ch. viii., p. 200.

made with such solemnity by both powers of both states of Mercland and Northumberland, which took up a very great part of England; and it is likely that it was made general to *all England*.'* This law of Offa, you will observe, then, carries us up the stream of history to a period before that of Ethelwulf,—to a period during the Heptarchy; and as Judge Blackstone intimates, in the passage I have before quoted, *Tithes were paid before this.* This statement is further confirmed by Burns, who says—speaking of the time of Offa,—'That *Tithes were before paid in England*, by way of offerings, according to the ancient usages and decrees of the Church, appears from the Canons of Egbert, Archbishop of York, about the year of 750; and from an epistle of Boniface, Archbishop of Mentz, which he wrote to Cuthbert, Archbishop of Canterbury, about the same time: and from the 17th Canon of the General Council of Calcuith, A.D. 787. But this law of Offa was that which gave the Church a *civil right* in them, by way of property and inheritance, and enabled the clergy to gather and recover them as *their legal due*, by coercion of the civil power.'* And it is further to be observed,

* Ibid, p. 201.
† Burns' Eccl. Laws, Nol. iii., p. 679.

that these documents to which Burns refers, speak of the payment of Tithes as then existing. Johnson, giving a further account, says, 'We cannot doubt but Tithes were paid in England at this time, and before. Boniface in the year 693 was twenty years of age, and he testifies that Tithes were paid in the English Church, in his letter to Cuthbert; and there is reason to believe that they were paid freely and fully, or else the King (Ina) who made so severe a law for paying the Church-scot, would have made a severer for paying Tithes, as some Kings did some hundred years after this, when the people's first fervour abated. The *Church-scot* was a new taxation, and therefore not readily paid. *Tithes were from the beginning, and therefore paid without repining.'* From the 17th Canon of Calcuith also, it would appear that although Tithes were customarily paid, yet such payment was popularly considered as a discharge from giving alms. This view was, however, reprobated in the Council, and men were enjoined to render not only the tenth, as already belonging to God, but also to seek His blessing by charitable gifts out of the nine portions that belonged to

* Johnson. Sub. ann. 693. See Soames Anglo-Saxon Church, p. 93.

themselves.* A similar view to this was evidently taken in Offa's law respecting Tithes, already alluded to. Augustine, the missionary, also about A.D. 600 received, in answer to certain questions propounded by him to Gregory the Great, instructions in pecuniary matters to follow the Roman usage. This usage enjoined the payment of Tithes, and carries us still further up the stream of time, and just agrees with what the learned Puritan, John Selden, says, who, as we have before stated, not only confesses, but proves out of ancient records that Tithes were paid to the Church before the end of the fourth century.†

St. Augustine, Bishop of Hippo (not the missionary to England above alluded to, but) one of the greatest fathers of the Church who lived more than two hundred years before the other Augustine, speaks very plainly about the payment of Tithes to the Church, telling men that they ought to separate something out of their yearly fruits, or daily income, and

* Soames, p. 117. Conc. Calc. Can. 17. Spelman i., 298; and Wilkins i., 150. Soames questions very much whether the quadripartite, or even the tripartite division of the Tithes ever became general in England, though it was recommended. See the preface to his Anglo-Saxon Church.

† Selden, pp. 35, 46.

O

that a tenth to a Christian was but a small proportion. Because it is said the Pharisees gave Tithes, 'I fast twice in the week, I give Tithes of all that I possess.' And our Saviour saith, 'Except your righteousness exceed the righteousness of the Scribes and Pharisees ye shall not enter into the kingdom of heaven.' But if he whose righteousness ye are to exceed give Tithes, and you give not a thousandth part, how can you be said to exceed him, whom you do not so much as equal.* Again, in another place, this same Augustine says, 'Our forefathers abounded in all things because they gave Tithes to God, and tribute to Cæsar; but now our devotion to God is sunk, the taxes of the State are raised upon us. We would not give God His part in the Tithes, and therefore the whole is taken away from us. The exchequer devours what we would not give to Christ.'† And from this passage it is also evident that Tithes were paid before the time of even this Augustine.

Now there is every reason to believe that what was early adopted by the Christians abroad,

---

* Aug. Com. on Psa. 146. Tom. viii. p. 698.
† Aug. Hom., tom. x, p. 201.

was followed out in this country. Even Selden says, 'Neither is it likely in those times, the custom in this island therein should differ from what was even uniformly received through those parts of Christendom, whereof we have the best testimony remaining. But if ancient authority were of credit Parish Churches expressly mentioned of about the time of 490 A.D., and endowed as at this day, might be found among the *Britons*. For when Dubritius was made Archbishop of South Wales, which they called *Dextralis Britannia*, and his see appointed at *Llandaff*, under Mauris, Prince of that Wales, divers Churches, with their endowment of Tithes, Oblations, and other profits were appropriated to him and his successors.'* Why does Mr. Miall keep back such statements as these? It were easy to mention other instances and passages from early writers, showing how general the payment of Tithes had become among all converts to Christianity. I will only give one more instance from earlier times as it refers to England, and a period before Augustine the missionary came. It is stated on the authority of Giraldus's Cambriensis, that when Germanus and

* Selden on Tithes, chap. ix., p. 209.

Lupus came over from the Continent, to assist the British Christians against the Pelagian heresy, they taught the ancient Britons 'to pay Tithes partly to the Bishop and partly to their baptismal Church.'*

"There is then abundance of evidence, you will perceive, to prove that Tithes were from a very early date paid in England, and that they must in the first instance have originated in the spontaneous liberality of the owners of the land, because there was at the first no civil law to compel the payment of these Tithes, and the payment, to a certain extent, depended upon the willingness of these several individuals. Thus the payment of Tithes must originally have been purely voluntary; but when it was found that too many individuals who inherited lands which were permanently charged with payment of Tithes, tried to evade the payment of what was due to the Church, it was then found necessary to invoke the highest power in the land to secure the payment of these Tithes generally as a permanent right of the Church. The right had been established, as it has been shown long before the close of the Heptarchy,

* See Comber on Tithes, p. 183.

and every law or charter relating to Tithes, afterwards made, enforced the payment; none of them originated Tithes. I trust, however, I shall not weary you with these statements and the proofs which I think it necessary to advance in behalf of the church's right to her Tithes, but if these were not thoroughly entered into we should gain but a superficial and incomplete comprehension of the subject."

Madam Britannia: "Oh no! you do not weary us, I assure you: I am much interested in researches of this kind, and especially in this case, as it will enable us the better to comprehend the matter, which must have a practical bearing and influence upon the legislation of the country, and is closely connected with the real welfare of the people; it is, therefore, of great moment to get to the bottom of such a subject as this, that we may be able to judge for ourselves about the right, and to uphold it, if it be necessary."

John Bull: "I must honestly confess, that I am pleased to hear the matter thoroughly argued, and have it once more firmly settled—one way or another—as the unsettling of it is hurtful to the country; we are, therefore, obliged to Mother Church for the information which she is at the trouble to afford us."

Mother Church: "And now as to the way in which Tithes originated. I have little doubt in my own mind, and I am bound to confess it,— because I see no wrong in it, even if it were done at the present time, but rather see in it a carrying out of God's plan and the Scriptural principle— that when the Gospel was first preached among the inhabitants of Great Britain, and as converts were made to Christianity, they were urged and enjoined to give a portion of their substance for the support of the Church and its ministers. God's ancient people, the Jews, they would be told, were enjoined to give a tenth portion of their substance to God's service, and, that if they who heard the Gospel desired to be acknowledged as God's people, they should not do less. This, no doubt, was often set before them as a duty, and their observance of it was regarded as a proof of their sincerity in embracing Christianity; not that they were to be content with merely giving the Tithe, but this at least was to be regarded as belonging o God, as His portion and not theirs, and that of the rest which they had they should also offer willingly.*

"The importance of making a permanent pro-

* See Selden, chap. iv. p. 36.

vision for the preachers of the Gospel was early recognized in England; and, that the Church might become settled in the land, so that they might enjoy the blessing of its ministrations, the early converts, besides making large grants of land in many instances, readily made a perpetual charge of Tithes upon their estates, which the Church should ever hereafter enjoy, and of which none of their successors to the property in future generations, who were not so well inclined to religion as themselves, might deprive the Church. Of course, in the first instance, whether it was done by the individual possessors of the soil, or by the sovereign when he made a grant of land to any of his followers with this condition,—this perpetual grant or charge of Tithes upon their estates was a voluntary matter. The land was theirs, and they could give, or withhold, such a grant, as many did; for the grant of Tithes was not effected all at once, and it was only after a number of years had elapsed, and social advantages became apparent to the owners of estates, that the Tithes became general throughout the country. Now, be it observed, whilst it was in their own hands it was theirs to give or withhold,—they were the lawful possessors, and none had a right to take even this tenth from them; but when it was given, not for one year only, but in perpetuity to the Church, and that in the most solemn and public manner, before many witnesses, then this tenth was no longer theirs, or their successors, to withhold from the Church. 'This,' as Sulivan says, 'created a permanent right in the Church, not by the force of any general law or canon, but from the special grant of the grantor, and the power he had to charge his lands.'* For no one can deny the right of the owner of land to make such a charge upon his property; or, that these tithes do not become the legal and valid property of the Church, when such grants have been sanctioned and apparently secured, as they have been, by the lawful authorities of the country."

Mother Church continued: "I think, moreover, it must be known to us all, from the ancient records of our history, that owing to the frequent invasions of this country by barbarous hordes,—devasting large tracts of territory,—the holding of property was very insecure, and continually changed hands. And it is not unreasonable to suppose,—and indeed history bears it out as a

* Sullivan's Lecture on the Constitution and Laws of England, Lec. ix.

fact,—that however the landmarks of property might be obliterated, and a redistribution of land at times found to be necessary among the followers of the conquerors, Christian kings and their nobles were anxious, and took great care that the Church should again have her Rights in property, as far as they could honestly determine them, when affairs were settled: and on any fresh adjustment of property Tithes were secured to the Church as a matter of justice. This I doubt not was the reason which led to Ethelwulf's grant or charter. We have a striking instance of this, moreover, in the life of Alfred the Great, Ethelwulf's son, when he admitted the Danes, whom he conquered, to settle as colonists in the Eastern Counties. Having agreed to receive baptism, these settlers were bound over, under a heavy penalty, to pay the liabilities or dues, from time immemorial fixed upon their several estates, and among these Tithes are named. Allusion is made to this by Selden also, who says, 'In the laws made between *King Alfred and Guthrun the Dane* (to whom the provinces of East Anglia and Northumberland were given to hold of the Crown), and renewed also between the same Guthrun and King Edward, son to Alfred, about the year 900, this occurs, . . as the old Latin translation hath it,

'*Si quis Decimate contra teneat, reddat Lashlite cum Dacis Witam cum Anglis.* Lashlite denotes the *Danish* common forfeiture, which, as it is thought, was in most offences 12 ores (that was commonly xx shillings, for xx pence made an ore commonly). The *English* common forfeiture, or the *Wite* was xxx shillings. The occurrence of these two names is frequent in Saxon laws, and it may seem by this, that some other law preceded for the payment of Tithes, or else that the Right of them was otherwise supposed clear.'* There is further evidence of this endeavour being continually made by the authorities of the realm to secure to the Church her Tithes, and more conclusive even, as we proceed down the stream of history."

Here Mother Church paused, for at this moment a usher appeared and intimated that luncheon was laid in the adjoining room. Madam Britannia invited them all, therefore, to partake of some refreshment, saying, that they would be better able to proceed with their discussion after their repast; for the subject they were considering was of that importance and interest that they had better continue it, whilst it was fresh in their minds.

* Selden, chap. viii., p. 203.

PART VI.

Upon returning again to the room where their discussion had been held,

The Lady from Threadneedle Street said, "I am glad our worthy friend has given us some explanation of the probable origin of the Tithe system in this country; and I would further ask, 'Is not *the great difference in the dimension of parishes*, and the singular manner in which the lands of one parish lie in respect to those of other parishes around, a kind of collateral evidence in support of what Mother Church has stated as to the origin of Tithes, and the Right of the Church to them? For, if the Tithes had been originally given by the State, or Council of the realm, or by the King, independently of the will of the owners, might we not reasonably have expected to find a more equal and systematic division of parishes than we now have? We should not have found (to judge of matters in an ordinary way) a parish of a few hundred acres lying close adjoining to another of as many thousand acres. There would, in all likelihood, have been some more even measurement—some nearer approach in size to each other, if such a grant or apportionment of Tithes had been given by the civil power in the first instance and at one time, as some suppose. But the fact that there is such a very great disproportion in the size or extent of the several parishes, and of the Tithes allotted to them, is a clear proof, I think, that the Tithes could not have been originally given as a national grant, and at one time, by the King, or council of the realm, independently of the several owners of property. Tithes can not, therefore, be regarded as a tax, which having been imposed by Parliament, may by Parliament be repealed without violating any right of the people. And further, this fact, which is apparent everywhere, throughout the length and breadth of the land, as to the unequal size of parishes, and the amount of Tithes attached to them severally, is a proof of the correctness of the views enunciated by our friend as to the origin of Tithes; it is a standing and lasting memorial in the land, everywhere visible, of the only reasonable account that can be given of it, viz., that the owners of property,—some of whom had small estates only, and others large estates,—assigned the Tithes of them severally to the Church to secure the ministrations thereof for themselves, their families, their dependents, and successors."

Mother Church: "Yes; this difference in the size and peculiar shape of the parishes strongly corroborates the view I have set forth; especially when taken in connection with *the existence of private patronage,* which still continues in the Church of England. For the additional fact of so many Advowsons—which gives the right of presentation to Church livings—being in the hands of private families, and chiefly those having landed property, can only be satisfactorily accounted for on the ground that the Tithes and Glebe were originally given by the owners of property; and that this right to present a clergyman to a living, subject to the approval of the Bishop, which has come down to their successors,—was originally granted, and held out as an inducement to former owners of the land, to make a settled provision for the clergyman that should be appointed."

Madam Britannia: "Might I ask whether there be any historical evidence of this?—for if so, it would greatly serve to establish what you have stated."

Mother Church: "Oh yes! and with your permission I shall be glad to furnish you with it. Theodore, who became Archbishop of Canterbury sixty-three years after Augustine died, (and *one hundred and eighty-seven years before the grant of Ethelwulf's charter,*) and to whom the Church of England is much indebted for uniting under one rule, the ancient British clergy and those of the communion of Rome introduced by Augustine, and constituting them as the clergy of an independent branch of the Church of Christ;—this Theodore, I say, 'besides providing for his adopted country an outline of ecclesiastical jurisdiction, and terms of religious conformity, appears to have been guided by a usage of his native Asia in planning the establishment of a parochial clergy. Under royal sanction, he followed Justinian, in offering the perpetual patronage of churches as an encouragement for their erection.' Soames, whose words I am quoting, in his History of the Anglo-Saxon Church, says, 'Opulent proprietors were thus tempted to supply the spiritual wants of their tenantry, and Bede records two instances in which this judicious policy proved effective. Theodore's

Oriental system had been, however, in operation for ages before every English estate of any magnitude had secured the benefit of a church within its boundary. This very lingering progress has thrown much obscurity about the origin of parishes. The principle of their formation will however, account for their unequal size, and for existing rights of patronage.'*

"The policy inaugurated by Theodore was approved and furthered by Athelstan, 'one of the wisest, most powerful, and most energetic of Anglo-Saxon princes,' who granted the rank of Thane, or Gentleman, to every such proprietor of the soil as would provide for his tenants a place of worship. In Johnson's translation of the Anglo-Saxon Chronicle the words are: 'If a churl thrived so as to have five hides of his own land, *a church*, a kitchen, a bell-tower, a seat, and an office in the king's court, from that time forward he was accounted equal in honour to a Thane.'†

"Thus we perceive that the dignity of Thane, or Gentleman, was open to the people among the Anglo-Saxons; and when one of the conditions

---

* Soames, pp. 85, 86.
† Spelman, Conc. i. 406.

was that a church should be built upon his property, we can have little doubt but that 'a wealthy aspirant of humble origin would be careful to prevent any deficiency in this particular from crossing his ambitious views! However small an estate was, its lord commonly would not rest contented without a church upon it. Nor often, says Soames, did he forbear to shew whose accommodation was first consulted, by placing the new erection close to his own home, although both the chief population, and the house provided for its minister, might be at some distance.' 'Parishes, therefore, owe their actual dimensions to no negligence or caprice, but to the accidental inequalities of private property.'*

"The Church's *dowry* of glebe had notoriously been settled upon it by some landowner, who likewise raised the fabric, and provided more effectually for the maintenance of its minister, *by resigning in his favour one-tenth of all that his own possessions around should hereafter produce.* Such public spirit justly demanded a suitable acknowledgment. None could be more so, than a freehold right of selecting, under proper control, that functionary who was to realize the liberal

* Soames, p. 3.

donor's pious intentions. This was nothing beyond an equitable return to an individual, who had not only provided his neighbours with a place of religious worship at his own expense, but had also rendered this liberality available to them, and to those who should come after them, by building a parsonage, by rendering inalienably a part of his own property as glebe, and *by burdening irredeemably the remainder.'** These words seem to me, my friends, very conclusive on this point, that the original boundaries of our parishes were determined in the main, by the extent of the estates of those who built and endowed churches on them, and that part of this endowment being the Tithes on the several estates for the permanent maintenance of the clergyman, the appropriation of it was sanctioned and approved by the authorities both in Church and State.

"This view of the matter is further confirmed by Selden, who cannot be accused of having any design of favouring the Church, but who gives some useful and reliable information as to the course of events, or the manner in which the Parochial system grew out of the Diocesan. He says, 'that in these primitive times of the English-

* Soames, p. 4.

Saxon Church, the Bishop and the whole Clergy of the Diocese were as one body living upon their endowments (bestowed on the Bishopric) and their treasure that came from the sundry places of devotion, whither some one or other of them, at the Bishop's appointment, was sent to preach the Word and minister the Sacraments; every Clerk having his dividend for his maintenance. Neither in these elder times, I think, did any of these Clergy or Chaplains usually reside elsewhere than with him at his Bishopric (as Deans and Chapters at this day) or in some Monasteries whence they might, as occasion required, at certain times go into those parishes which were distinguished only for several functions of those Chaplains, lest want of such distinction might sooner have caused also a want of a special discharge of this or that cure.' And then he continues further on, 'But afterwards, when devotion grew firmer, and most Laymen of fair estate desired the country residence of some Chaplains, that might be always ready for Christian instruction among them, their families and adjoining tenants; oratories and churches began to be built by them also: and being hallowed by the Bishops, were endowed with peculiar maintenance from the Founders, for the Incumbents that should there only reside. Which maintenance, with all other Ecclesiastical profits that came to the hands of every several Incumbent (in regard, that now the Lay-founder had, according to the territory of his demesnes, tenancies, or neighbouring possessions, made and assigned both the limits within which the holy function was to be exercised, and appointed the persons that should repair to the Church, and offer there, as also provided a special salary for the performance) was afterwards also restrained from that common Treasure of the Diocese, and made the only revenue, which became perpetually annexed to the Church of that Clerk who received it. Neither was it wonder that the Bishops should give way to such restraint. For had they denied that to Lay-founders, they had given no small cause also of restraining their devotion. Every man, questionless, would have been the unwillinger to have specially endowed the Church, founded for the holy use of him, his family, and tenants, if withal he might not have had the liberty to have given his Incumbent, there resident, a special and several maintenance; which could not have been, had the former community of the clergy's revenue still remained. Out of these Lay-foundations chiefly, doubtless came those kind of Parishes which at this day are in every Diocese. Their differences in quantity being originally out of the difference of the several circuits of the demesnes or territories possessed by the Founder.'* The very character of our Parishes being so diversified in size, then, bears ample witness, and is a standing monument of the munificence of the owners of property in the early English Church, and that the Tithes appropriated by them to their several churches were confirmed and secured to the Church as an inalienable right in the strongest possible manner. But to return to the thread of our evidence;—

"As we come down the stream of history from Ethelwulf's and Alfred's. time, we find constant decisions made in the Councils of the Realm to support the Church in obtaining her due right of Tithes. Thus,

"In *Athelstane's reign*, the legislative assembly holden at Grately, enacted that Tithes should be strictly paid, not only on crops, but upon live stock.†

"In *Edmund's reign*, another legislative assembly, held in London, again enjoined the payment of Tithes.‡

* Selden, pp. 254, 259, 260.
† Spelman Conc. i. 396. Wilkins, i. 205.
‡ Spelman, i. 420. Wilkins, i. 214.

"Notwithstanding these enactments, it was still found that the Church suffered great loss from the avarice of worldly men, and the legislature was accordingly driven, *in Edgar's reign*, to compel by civil penalties, the due discharge of that claim to which the land was liable. It was enjoined that the Tithe of stock be paid at Pentecost, and the Tithes of the fruits of the earth by the Equinox, and if not then paid, seizure might be made by the joint action of the King's and Bishop's reeves, and a heavy fine exacted.*

"*In Ethelred's reign*, the payment of Tithe was again enjoined, and a more exact method laid down, viz., that the produce of every tenth acre was to be rendered, as the plough went.†

There are other enactments that might be noticed, especially those in *Canute's reign*,‡ and *Edward the Confessor's*.§

"But without troubling you with the exact words of these, or even of those before named,¶ we come

* Spelman, i. 444.   Wilkins, i. 245.
† Spelman i., 531.   Wilkins i., 295.
‡ Selden, pp. 223, 224.
§ Ibid, pp. 224, 225.
¶ The very words of nearly all these are to be found in Selden's viii. chap., first in the old Saxon characters—then in old Latin, so any one may look into the matter further if he desires to do so.

to a great landmark in the history of our country, viz., the reign of William, the Conqueror. When this Sovereign at last found himself settled on the throne of England, he commissioned twelve learned and able men to ascertain, as far as they were able, what were the laws of the country during the reign of Edward the Confessor, and these being ascertained, he, at the express desire of the people, re-enacted and consolidated as the common law of the land. Among these are the injunctions or laws respecting Tithes, for after certain specifications it is there laid down that 'whosoever shall withhold this tenth part shall by the justice of the King and Bishop, be forced to payment of it if needs be.'*

"In tracing the history of Tithes downwards from the time of the Norman Conquest there is most abundant testimony to its being fully acknowledged as a valid Right of the Church, by the legislature; I need, however, only be brief, for I do not wish to burden you with more evidence than is necessary to show you that it has been acknowledged all along. Henry I., Stephen, and Henry II. were each required to confirm and main-

* Hoveden's Annals, p. 602.   Spelman, p. 620.

tain these statutes of the realm, which confirmed the Right of Tithes to the Church.*

"In Edward I. and Edward III. reigns there are several Acts regulating the payment of Tithes, all of which more or less testify that they belong to the Church.†

"In Henry VIII. and Edward VI. reigns there were several Acts passed relating to Tithes. It is notorious that during these reigns many Tithes were alienated from the Church. But whilst the Tithes thus seized upon, on the dissolution of the Monasteries, were secured to the Sovereign and his patentees, upon whom they had been bestowed,—those that remained to the church, were still secured to her by legislative enactments, as they had been aforetime.‡

* Selden, p. 226-228.
† Selden, p. 232-241.

‡ It is worthy of observation to notice how even Henry VIII., through whom the Church lost so much of her property, confirmed the right of certain Tithes to the Church, which have since his days been lost to the Church, owing to the State not giving the Church sufficient protection against the pillage practised by great men. Thus 'by the Acts of 27 Hen. VIII. c. 21, and 37 Hen. VIII. c. 12, and the decree made upon them, the citizens and inhabitants of London, and the liberties were commanded to pay their Tithes to the Parsons, Vicars, and Curates of the City, according to a rate of the rents of their houses ; that is, two shillings and ninepence for every pound, and that if no rent be reserved, the Tithe should be

"Since the Reformation, in various reigns, many Acts have been passed relating to Tithes—some of which have proved detrimental, in no little degree, to the Church's interests, whereby the Church has lost hold of some of her Tithes; but the great fact has all along been acknowledged by the legislature of the country, and is so at this present moment, that Tithes, unless they were impropriated, or had become void in some particular instances by law, are of right belonging to the Church and must be paid; and the fact is still duly paid, according to what their houses had been last letten for, and according to that also, are owners bound to pay.' (Solden, p. 243.) It is a curious history to trace out how the Church lost so much of her property even since Hen. VIII's day. The days succeeding this were days of great tribulation to the Church, though she was eventually happily able to throw off the yoke and corruptions of Popery.

The people of the city of Canterbury and its suburbs had likewise to pay two shillings and ninepence in the pound out of their rents for Tithe. So also had the people of Coventry, and some parishes in Middlesex, Essex, Kent, and Surrey.

An award also was made in King Charles I's. reign settling two shillings in the pound out of the rents of houses for the maintenance of the parochial clergy.

If those Tithes, which were in lieu of land Tithes, had been retained to the Church in all our cities and large towns, what a large provision would have been made for the spiritual necessities of these populous places; and probably the rents would have been no higher han they are at present.

further patent that they have been all along claimed and paid as a lawful debt, or charge upon property.

"And now I trust you will bear with me a little longer whilst I endeavour to sum up the evidence I have laid before you."

Madam Britannia : "Certainly! for we are, I assure you, deeply indebted for the pains you have been at in laying this matter so fully before us."

Mother Church : "Thank you. And, first, all this evidence proves what a solid and well attested foundation the Right of Tithes rests upon; as it is not only one of the most ancient, but one so frequently acknowledged and ratified by the fundamental charters of the kingdom. And here I shall again take leave to bring before you the words of the learned lawyer, John Selden, as very applicable to the point. He says, 'The laws of before, as well as of after the Norman Conquest (as it is vulgarly called) are here gathered [*i.e.* in his viii. chap.], and are perhaps equally observable, as the rest, in the consequent of a *general* consecration of Tithes to the Church in England. For neither were the Laws formerly made abolished by that conquest, although by law of war, regularly all Rights and Laws of the place conquered, be wholly subject to the conqueror's will. For as this of the Norman, not only the conqueror's will was not declared that the former laws should be abrogated (and until such declaration, laws remain in force, by opinion of some, in all conquests of Christians against Christians,) but also the ancient and former laws of the kingdom were confirmed by him. For in his 4th year, by the advice of his Baronage, he summoned to London *Omnes Nobiles sapientes et lege sua cruditos, ut eorum leges et consuetudines audiret*, as the words are of the book of Lichfield, and afterwards confirmed them, as it is further also related in Roger of Hoveden. Those *lege sua cruditi*, were common lawyers of that time, as Godric and Alfwin were then also, who are spoken of in the book of Abingdon to be, *Legibus patriæ optime instituti*, &c.'* Now the argument that I shall found upon what I have hitherto stated, and the evidence that has been advanced is this, that the Church's Right to her Tithes does not rest simply upon one or two charters in the olden Saxon times, or the forced enactments of some arbitrary Saxon Sovereign; but upon a Right obtained by grants and inheritance from the original owners and possessors of the soil, and such as

* Selden's Review, p. 482.

has been continually and repeatedly acknowledged as lawfully belonging to the Church by the legislature of the country in successive reigns for more than a thousand years. Moreover, if there had been any doubt as to the Church's Right to Tithes in earlier times (which does not appear, further than what we might expect to find in men withholding what was due,) the matter seems to have been fully set at rest in the reign of William the Conqueror. For when a large redistribution of property took place among his followers, and he, as sovereign, granted fresh titles to the new owners, and confirmed the title of others, after a careful survey of the country by the royal commissioners appointed for this purpose, the Right of the Church to her Tithes also, as it has been shown was fully acknowledged and confirmed; so that not only long before, from time immemorial, but from this re-investigation and re-settlement of Titles to property after the Norman Conquest, it was satisfactorily proved that one-tenth of the property belonged to the Church, and only nine-tenths belonged to the owner or landlord; or rather, he was only owner or landlord to the extent of nine-tenths of the land he had, and must pay what was due to the Church for the remaining tenth.

" And if anything more was wanting to confirm and permanently settle the Church's Right to her Tithes, we have it laid down in the Magna Charta, that great bulwark of the people's Rights and Liberties. For in addition to the first clause, which runs thus, 'Know ye that we by the grace of God, &c. . . by the advice of our honoured fathers, and by the advice of other lieges have in the *first* place granted to God, and confirmed by this our present Charter, for us, and for our heirs for ever, that the Church of England shall be free, and shall enjoy its rights and franchises entirely and fully,'—there is this other clause, which secured to the people of England the safe possession and inheritance of their property, and which applies to the Church as well, '*that no man shall be disseized of his freehold, but by the judgement of his peers, and by the due course of law.*' It was the maintenance of this charter that has preserved the humblest and weakest in the land, against the strongest and highest; so that not even the King or any of the powerful Nobles might seize upon the property of another, or injure anyone; and I ask, can it be well for the people, to see this fundamental principle of our constitution, to which they are so deeply indebted, ruthlessly set aside, by suffering such an invasion of the Church's Right, as to permit her to be defrauded of her Tithes? Certainly not! Their interest lies in maintaining it.

Thus in times past have the possessions of the Church been secured to her, tied, and bound up with the safe possession of property by the rightful owners. And however much property has changed hands since these times,—whether by inheritance, by grant, or by purchase,—only nine-tenths of the said property was legally obtained, except in those cases where, by subsequent legal enactments, exemptions were made, or some composition was fixed upon. The Right of the Church to her Tithes is therefore as it were embedded and deeply rooted in the very constitution of our country, and the legal inheritance of property. The Church's title then, is one of the oldest, and best attested that can be produced. None can show an older title, or a better, or one more generally acknowledged, unless it be that of the Crown. The Church has had a prescriptive enjoyment of them for some hundreds of years before the Conquest, and since. And notwithstanding this long possession can prove a good title to them,—that she came fairly by the Tithes at the first, their being freely given to her, and acknowledged by the Sovereign (who as our best lawyers say, had then all the land of England in demesne. (Coke on Lit. : I. ch. 9, sec. 73), with the free consent and desire also of all the great lords and possessors in the kingdom, declared in the assembled council of the realm. And, for the better and more secure possession of this Right it has been confirmed by divers Acts of Parliament; nearly every King's reign bearing witness to it.

There are a certain class of men in the country who look with a greedy, covetous eye upon these ancient possessions of the Church, and agitate the country to seize upon them. They ridicule any fear of danger to the inheritance of property, or harm to the country, by this unsettling and uprooting one of the most ancient institutions of the land, the fibres of which run throughout the country and intersect every portion; but who, with an honest and reflecting mind, can view the history of England and the evidence in support of the Church's title to Tithes, and will not justly fear that it would shake the very framework of society and the settled constitution of our land to their very foundation, and be the beginning of a reign of additional bitterness, perplexity and disturbance, such as we have not lately seen in England, but which has of late been too frequently witnessed, and felt to the very core, in some of the nations of the Continent. Men accustomed to look at the result of actions, and who have studied the ultimate consequences that flow from great changes, affecting the moral and spiritual welfare of the country mentioned in history, know full well, that sooner or later there would be a fearful retribution, vastly affecting the peace and prosperity and stability of the country.

Moreover, it would be a wanton, despotic, and unjust act of tyranny towards a large portion of the community, who were well affected to the constitution, and deeply interested in the wellbeing of the country; for I speak now, not merely of the clergy, but of the laity in the Church of all classes, who are benefited by her ministrations. And to upset all this vast system, so well arranged, so fruitful for good, amid even its imperfections and shortcomings, and tending in so many ways materially to promote virtue, diminish crime, and alleviate the ills of poverty;—to upset all this extensive machinery for good, or at least wofully impair it, would be little short of madness, and culpable recklessness in the statesmen of our country; and it would appear, that notwithstanding they might do this at the instigation of and to please a few, (for they are not many compared with those who would otherwise be affected by the change) noisy politicians, and restless, clamorous, discontented sectaries, they may try in vain to satisfy and please them.

And what good would it do? None, that I can see; but much harm; for whilst it would not content those who are urging on the cry, it would cause a deep and lasting wound, which would not be soon healed, to a large section of the commonwealth who are at the present staunch supporters of the constitution, and the interests of the country.

Or again, who is hurt or injured by the continuance of Tithes to the Church? None that I know of! Certainly not those who are so ready to cry out against it,—not the landlords,—not the tenants, —not the poor, who would really be the greatest sufferers by taking them away. If a man buys an estate, he now usually buys only nine-tenths of the land, the remaining one-tenth still belonging to the Church: or if he inherits property, he in most cases only inherits nine-tenths, the one-tenth still belonging to the Church. And what wrong is done to him in either case if he only gets nine-tenths of the rent, and the clergyman of the parish the one-tenth? Or what wrong to the tenant, who if he did not pay the one-tenth to the Church, must pay it to the landlord?

Moreover, the landlord or owner in such cases does not pay the taxes of the country on the one-tenth, he is only charged on the nine-tenths; the legislature of the country thereby recognising the one-tenth as the valid inheritance or right in the property belonging to the Church, and charges her with her proportion of the taxes which are due,—and which she also pays; the which is a standing testimony that this title to the one-tenth in the property is still regarded by the civil authorities of the country as rightly owned by the Church.

Further, if you will only consider the matter awhile, the payment of Tithes is so contrived that it can never be hard upon *the poor;* and yet the poor have an equal right with the rich to the services of the Clergyman who is partly maintained by the Tithes; they often regard him as, and find him to be, their friend in their hour of need: so that it is really to the peeple's interest to preserve the Tithes intact to the Church.

But further, no man ought to call it a burden to give every one their own; the interest of the one-tenth does not belong to the landlord, nor to the tenant, nor to the State, but to the Church, and it ought to be given to the Church without the least demur as hers, by all that is right. To withhold it is but knavery and wrong-doing: for no other person or body of men can make any just claim upon it but the Church.

If Tithes were taken from the Church, there is no reason why they would not return to the lords of the soil; *the tenants* would not benefit by it, for if Tithes were taken off, the landlords, as we have just said, would want so much more rent in proportion; nor would *the labourer* on the property gain any advantage; it would be chiefly the rich, (who already have enough) that would in the end be benefited by doing away with the Tithe system.

Nor are *the Clergy*, as a body, overpaid, that the Tithes which remain to the Church should be taken from her. This is far from being the case, as it has been shewn on a former occasion; and as facts abundantly testify, they are much underpaid, considering their education, and the price which things are now at; for as a whole, they do not get sufficiently paid, and in many cases they can hardly, with the greatest economy, 'keep the wolf from the door.' Moreover, the Church is at the present time short of funds to prosecute her work as she desires to do, and has to go begging throughout the country to meet the increasing demands, and to supply the growing religious necessities of the times.

And then again, if Tithes were taken away from the Church, one of two things would happen, either the great mass of our poor would to a great extent be left without religious instruction, for as we have before shewn when speaking of other endowments of the Church, they are not in a position to support a minister properly educated; or, some new maintenance for the clergy must be obtained from the people; and as the latter is not likely to happen, the result of the former alternative would be to leave the people to lapse, in no little degree, into heathenism or atheism, the bitter fruits whereof would be reaped by our children, if not by ourselves.

Wherefore then, why not adhere to 'the old way' which God Himself choose, and which our prudent and pious ancestors—or rather the early possessors of the soil—adopted, settled, and handed down to us? Not to enter again upon the dangers and difficulties, the great disquietude and many inconveniences that would arise from such a change which the doing away of Tithes would involve, we, as a nation, will never be able to hit upon, or agree in, any more equal or easy way than that of Tithes. No system but what has its inequalities and inconveniences; this perhaps has the fewest, and such as can be easily rectified, if sanctioned by the legislature.

I have now finished what I have to say upon the subject, and must sincerely thank you all for listening so patiently to my defence of the Church's right to her Tithes."

Madame Britannia: "Nay indeed, I think we must all thank you, my venerable friend, for the clear and intelligible manner in which you have brought this matter before us. It is astonishing how much the records of history, when fairly set before us, not only serve to disperse the haziness and apparent uncertainty which hangs over a matter which has been so much misrepresented, but enable us to understand it more perfectly, and to see our way in it. To my mind, the evidence and the arguments you have adduced, should set the matter at rest, for I cannot conceive what more right our friend here, Mr. Bull, has to the nine-tenths of the rent which he receives from his tenants, than the Church has to her one-tenth."

John Bull : "Nor do I, I must candidly confess, after all the evidence and arguments I have listened to. For the Church seems to have just as good a right and title, if not better, to her portion, as I have to mine."

The Old Lady from Threadneedle Street : "Before we close the subject, I have, with your leave, one or two observations to make. I doubt not, but that if those who cry out so much about the Church enjoying her right to Tithes were themselves in possession of them, they would be the most strenuous supporters of the right, and would severely condemn those who wanted to do away with them. And in corroboration of this, it is a singular fact, worthy of note, that both the Presbyterian and Independent ministers during the time of the Commonwealth were most anxious to receive the Tithes, and most zealous in defending the payment of them. Both sets of "Godly Ministers" kept a sharp look out after them. In A.D. 1644 they got an ordinance made by the Lords and Commons assembled in Parliament, ' *For the true payment of Tithes*, and other such duties, according to the laws and customs of the realm.' And several such like ordinances were made about this time.

"Even Mr. Pryn himself argues very forcibly for their continuance in his 'Gospel plea for Tithes.' It is hardly consistent then, in those who profess to be the successors of these 'godly ministers' to oppose the enjoyment of Tithes by the Church, who is the legal owner of them. But it makes all the difference when they do not enjoy them.

"It is however satisfactory to know that there are some honest Dissenters, even in the present day, who candidly acknowledge the Church's Right to her Tithes and other endowments: and they are men too who have had the opportunity, and taken pains to look carefully into the question, and are therefore qualified to form an opinion, and to speak, with some knowledge, on the matter. Thus, Mr. Horace Mann, the compiler of the Religious Worship Census, said some years ago in his remarks (p. 4) that, 'upon the erection of a Church, or the foundation of a religious establishment, it became the custom—probably in imitation of a practice which appears to have prevailed in nearly every age, and every country in the world—for *the founder to devote a tenth of all his property to purposes of religion and charity. Tithes thus appear to have had their origin in voluntary payments*, and as such they were doubtless very generally rendered in the early periods of Anglo-Saxon rule.'

"Mr. Toulman Smith also, an eminent barrister among the Dissenters, stated in his evidence before a select committee of the House of Lords, February 16, 1860, 'I find by many of the old records, that it is clear that *the whole of the present endowments of the Church were voluntary endowments.* I can show that *the endowments* upon which the Church subsists *were endowments originally given by private individuals* for a specific maintenance of a Church for the people.' Again, after alluding to a document in Edward III.'s reign, he says, 'This proves the same thing as the records I have already quoted, namely, that the endowments of the Church were gifts by individuals, and not made by the State.' Another observation of his is also worthy of notice; he says, 'The connection of the Church with the State exists quite as much as to all Nonconformist endowments as it does to the Church endowments; and that *both one and the other have equally the protection of the law;* as has been illustrated in the case of Lady Hewley's charity and many others. It is notorious that the law interferes as stringently to maintain an endowment whether it be for a Dissenting form of worship, or for the Church of England; the latter being a Church for the people, and not a sect.'

"There are other evidences of a similar character from Dissenters, but these, I think, will suffice to corroborate the statements already advanced."

Madam Britannia: "Such disinterested testimony coming from those who cannot be charged with any prejudice is certainly very conclusive, and must serve greatly to strengthen the Church's Right to her endowments."

John Bull: "I am quite of your opinion, Madam; and I shall go away fully satisfied and prepared to uphold the Church in her Rights, after all I have heard."

Madam Britannia: "I think there can be little need now to discuss the Right of the Church to her *more recent endowments*, for it is too absurd to imagine that the property she has acquired within the last two hundred years or so does not of right belong to her."

The Old Lady from Threadneedle Street: "And yet even this property is brought in question by some wily politicians and the determined foes of the Church. A Dissenting minister writes thus in a little work before alluded to, 'It ought not to be omitted from our view of this subject (endowments) that of late years a large amount of property has become Church property by private donation. Those who give to the Church of England give to a National Institution—in fact, to the nation—and they must accept in regard to their gifts all the conditions to which Church property is subject.' And, again, further on he says, 'The nation may hereafter deal with Church property and *with recent gifts*, to which we are referring and which are part of it, as may appear expedient.'* But, still it is fair to add, that he thinks the opinion of the leaders of the Liberation Society is, that whatever Church property has accrued by private gift since the Reformation, ought to be secured for ever to the Episcopal Church. Again, a person, now holding a position of great importance, says in a paper read at Sion College, January 20, 1870, 'If men give property to the Church and the Church takes it, the property is given and taken subject to State control, on State terms, upon conditions laid down from time to time by the State, and liable to be altered by the power

* Church Property : What is it, and whose ? p. 15.

which has laid them down.' And this sentence is laid hold of by the Church's foes. But I would ask, is not *all property* subject to State control in a greater or less degree, and must be held on State terms, upon conditions laid down from time to time by the State? And though the State is more especially the guardian of Church property, and thereby has more intimate transactions with it than most other properties, yet has it no right, morally, to make any conditions inimical to the interests of the Church, any more than it has to deal thus with other properties in the country. What I complain of, therefore, is this, that such like insinuations about Church property tend to make men think that Church property is more insecure than other properties, which is but to pander to men holding theories hostile to the Church. Whereas, I hold it, that since the State is the guardian of Church property, and has received this trust from times long past, it is the more bound, and not the less, to protect it and secure it to the Church, and to transmit this trust unimpaired to future generations: and the more so because it is employed for the welfare of the people. That the State has not always done this, is no argument against its duty to do this, any more than when a man has failed two or three times in a plain duty, it is an argument in favour of his failing again in it. Such enunciations therefore ought to be severely reprobated, by whomsoever they may be uttered."

Madam Britannia: "I quite agree with you, that such sentiments ought not to be set forth, for they much unsettle men's minds, leading them to imagine that the State is not to be trusted any more with fresh gifts to the Church, and that some day or another she may prove unfaithful, and, to use a common expression, 'sack' it all. Let it the rather be well settled in the minds of all Englishmen that the State will always endeavour to do, and uphold, what is right, in matters relating to the Church, as well as to other bodies, and that she will maintain and secure the Church in her ancient endowments, as well as her more recent ones, as she would that of other owners to their property."

John Bull: "Such sentiments are worthy of you, madam, and I doubt not the country will endorse them, and support you in your desire to do right to all. To listen to what some people say they would make us believe that wrong was right, and right was wrong, and that we did not know whether we stood upon our heads or our heels; but this kind of talk must end in smoke, and get dispersed, though for the while it obscures men's visions."

The Old Lady from Threadneedle Street: "It has been calculated that within the last fifty years no less a sum than seventy-five millions have been voluntarily contributed to the Church,* but whether the sum be less or more, we care not, for it is not essential to our purpose to name the exact sum; it is the principle that we contend for, that the Church shall have and enjoy her own, and remain as securely, and as undisturbed in her possession of them, whether they were given long ago, or only lately, as any other religious body in the country."

John Bull: "It is my opinion that the enemies of the Church would fain take away all that she has, even her recent endowments, and that they would strip her bare and turn her out penniless

* Another calculation makes it considerably more. Mr. H. Cecil Raikes, M.P., is reported to have stated at the late Church Congress held at Bath, that during the past forty years £2,000,000 annually had been sunk in permanent investments for the benefit of the Church, and not less than £1,300,000 had been subscribed in addition annually for purely parochial purposes. If, then, we calculate the latter sum to have been sunk in current expenses, the former sum will give £80,000,000 for only forty years.

into the world, if it were not from the fear that people would cry 'shame upon them;' and that they might be called upon to give up their own possessions as well, if this were done; and therefore they try to make it appear that they mean to be gracious towards the Church—would not despoil her of what she has recently acquired—thinking no doubt also that they may be the more likely to rob her of her ancient endowments. But it is all of a piece with their unscrupulous audacity. And things are not as they should be in the country, when one portion of the country is kept in fear that they will be despoiled of their lawful and ancient possessions by another portion; and I verily believe that a civil war would break out did the legislature consent to such a deed. But I have great hopes that the good sense of the people will lead them steadily to set their faces against any such attempt. Still it seems to me, if I may be allowed to speak my mind, that with such a constitutional government as we have in England, such an event should not even be entertained, as the right of all classes and societies should be firmly respected and upheld."

Madam Britannia : " Well said, my friend; but I fancy there is a covert reproof for me in your words."

The Lady from Threadneedle Street: "Endowments are usually made by wealthy persons for the special benefit of the people, or their poor neighbours. But who will like to endow institutions when it is uncertain what will be done with the money in fifty years time? What encouragement is there for liberal-minded men to secure some advantage to the people by an endowment if government admit the principle that such endowments may be diverted from the object designed by the donor? If this reckless interference with the ancient endowments of the country be once permitted it will be one of the heaviest blows that can be given to those kindly feelings and acts which are beginning to revive again in these days, whereby men of large hearts provide more efficient means to encourage learning, to alleviate the hard lot of the poor and outcasts, and to enable them to worship God, in the beautiful sanctuary of His house, as well as their neighbours who can pay for their minister. If endowments become practically hurtful or useless, this is a different matter; but so long as they are useful and advantageous to the country, there ought not, for one moment, to be any fear of their absolute security and continuance.

A bequest, or the gift of a donor ought to be held, under these circumstances, sacred and inviolable: for it is the disposal of that which the law allows to be his own, and for an object also which the law permits and sanctions. Ere the first French revolution had fully broken out Robespierre cried out in the Constituent Assembly, 'Is a man to be allowed to dispose of the land he cultivated, after he himself has gone to dust?' and we know the result which such revolutionary sentiments led to, and will again lead to, if allowed to gain currency among us. No, no! Such sentiments as these must receive no encouragement from good men, or from those in authority. The will of a pious founder, or the gift of a noble heart, ought to be the more securely protected after death than in life: for the will of the dead is a duty imposed upon the living, and it is ever the province of a wise and stable government to see that it is faithfully observed.

That endowments have largely increased, during the last fifty or sixty years, for other objects, as well as for the Church, is a most hopeful sign of a growing sympathy existing among us, which greatly tends to strengthen the bands of society; and it is something more, it is a sign, notwithstanding all the foolish and bitter talk there has been, that there is still great confidence in the country—a growing confidence that the State will uphold and maintain the endowments that have been made, whether those of late years, or those in days long ago. And great care should be exercised that this confidence be not shaken or abused by those in authority."

Madam Britannia: "In a free country like ours, and where there is such a diversity of opinions, some latitude of speech and action must be allowed. Besides it is the duty of the Legislature to interfere in correcting evils, and regulating existing rights, so that one be no ways injurious to another; and that the rights of all may be protected and promoted. For in the constant changes of time there is a necessity for readjusting rights, and fixing upon the best way in which the several rights of individuals, families, and societies, should be exercised in order to help rather than hinder each other in their common development. And then further, by reason of the avarice and other passions of men, there is also a necessity of protecting by force, the rights and interests of all from every unjust and violent attack, whether from within or from without. The Civil power must first of all guard against having its own authority injured or weakened, and then, whilst guarding all other rights from harm, promote their efficiency, or afford facility to the full development and use of them."

The Old Lady from Threadneedle Street: "So far I think you are right, but in applying what you say, I think you strengthen what our friend, Mr. Bull, says with regard to Church property; for surely the Church, as well as any other religious body, should have her Rights protected and promoted; and there ought to be no fear in the country that the State will ever sanction or encourage their overthrow, but a prevailing trust that the State will act uprightly, and rather shrink and withdraw from in anywise impairing, absorbing, or trampling upon the Rights of the Church."

Madam Britannia: "The sovereign power in a country, in whatever form it exists, or however it has been derived, has *its limits*, I allow, as well as *its duties;* it cannot legitimately injure, or encroach upon, existing rights, whether they be the rights of the individual, the rights of the family, the rights of the Church, or the rights of voluntary associations; for these are prior to the existence of State power, which has indeed been called into existence, and is upheld, for the very purpose of regulating and defending these several rights, and clear the way to the free exercise of them. Every individual has, by his own natural right, the power of associating himself with his fellows, so long as he does it openly and for objects which are not subversive of morality and the public peace. And in like manner all other rights are to be acknowledged and maintained. And to infringe upon the rights of individuals, separately or collectively, either in restraining their liberty, beyond what necessity requires, or taking from any of them what of natural right belongs to them, is an abuse of power, and a frustration of the object for which civil power is intrusted to the State."

Mother Church : " It is much to be desired that these views respecting the duties and limits of the civil or legislative power were better understood and regarded : for if there was a sincere desire to act upon them, as I doubt not it is your wish, Madam, there would be little difficulty, not only in securing to the Church what is her own, but in affording facilities for correcting abuses, and granting more liberty of action within the Church than at present exists."

John Bull: " I am decidedly against any separation of Church and State, mind you. I once thought it would be necessary, and must come before long; but I don't think so now. It is not only not necessary, but it would be an evil day for this country should it ever take place: that I can see perfectly well; but this is not your design, Madam, I think."

Mother Church: "Oh, no! I am opposed to it, as much as yourself, as you may judge from what I have already said on a previous occasion. But what I mean is, that whilst still keeping the connection up in full vigour,—the Sovereign, through her government, still holding supreme authority in all matters Ecclesiastical,—the Church should be allowed greater liberty and freedom of action; as for instance, in the election of Bishops. Why might not the Queen be permitted to issue a *congé d'èlire* to the Clergy and Laity of a Diocese upon a vacancy occurring, to elect a Bishop, not indicating the person they must choose, but requiring that the election be approved by the Sovereign in Council, and the Bishop elect to pay homage as at present.*

---

* The wording of the Act of Parliament under which the Sovereign nominates the Bishops to be elected, shows that this *is not a positive duty*, but *optional;* as if to be exercised only in cases of need, as at the time of the Reformation or the Revolu-

Too many who argue upon this matter respecting the liberty of the Church, think that they must either keep things as they are—*i.e.*, withholding liberty of action from the Church, which is accorded to other religious bodies, and which is most desirable to develope her well-being; or, they think that the connection of Church and State must be broken up, and the Church be under no control from the State, from which anarchy is to ensue. I wish I could get all these persons to see and understand that all the *liberty* which is needed for the Church may be safely, and more safely, exercised *in connection with the State*, than not;—the State still having the power to interfere whenever it be necessary, in every point as it does now; but only when some apparently sufficient cause may be shewn for this interference. This I believe to be the true principle of liberty, and more in accordance with the principles of the British Constitution than that which is at present exercised towards the Church."

tion. See 31 Henry VIII. c. 19.20, where immediately after the clause for the Submission of the Clergy, there is another whereby the King is permitted to nominate the Bishops. At every voidance the King and his heirs, "*may* grant . . . a license under the great seal . . to an election . . with a letter missive, containing the name of the person which they shall elect and choose."

Madam Britannia: "Thank you. This matter must be more fully considered before long. I cannot but hold it to be dangerous suddenly to wrench assunder the union of Church and State; the two having grown up side by side, and been entwined together so long: still I do not see why the Church should not be considered capable of managing her own affairs, in strict conjunction with the State; the State having a direction in, and approval of all that is done. Surely it is better for a husband, and it leaves the husband more at liberty too to attend to other matters, and it worries him less, to suffer his wife to attend to matters in her own department,—appointing her own household servants, ordering things for the house, settling disputes among the servants, arranging household economies as occasion may require,—with the sanction and advice of the husband when needful,— than to treat her as an incapable person in such matters. Such a course seems most natural, as well as rational, and wise in many ways. And to allow the wife this liberty of action, surely it is not necessary to separate. This would be as bad, if not worse than· to treat her as incapable. So I trust we shall yet have statesmen that will rise equal to the occasion, and able to guide and settle affairs in such a manner that whilst the Church may be allowed her true liberty, as her natural right, her union with the State may be preserved in the strictest integrity.

"But tell us before we part, for I know not when we shall meet again,—how the Legislature could facilitate reforms in the Church with regard to the sale of private patronage, for I feel that the scandal which is caused thereby at times ought to be remedied without delay?"

Mother Church : "Keeping before us the duties laid down of the legislative power, the shortest and best way to prevent scandal would be to pass a short bill, to prevent the public sale of livings in private patronage; and that whenever a private patron desired to part with his patronage, there should be a Church body in each Diocese,—representatives chosen equally from the Clergy and Laity, with the Bishop at their head,—who should be empowered to give to such private patrons what the Living would bring at the present market price, which is often not more than from six to seven years purchase : and that they should have powers to sell lands, and invest securely, rearrange the income of these Livings, and have the appointment of Clergymen upon a vacancy. This is but a very rough and brief sketch of the way in which the Legislature might facilitate a reform in the Sale of Livings in private hands; I have given much thought to this matter, but as time presses, I trust what I have said will sufficiently indicate my views on the question."

Madam Britannia: "Once more let me thank you. The discussions we have had together so far on Church Politics have not been lost upon me; and will bear fruit, I think."

Some inquiry was now made as to when they should meet again to discuss further some of the other Rights of the Church, which had been previously named. They all felt that the consideration of them must ere long come to the front, and that it was very desirable to discuss them fully and calmly by themselves. Nothing definitely, however, was settled, and it was therefore left open for them to meet as they should afterwards find fitting opportunity.

There was now a general movement to leave, and having wished each other a cordial 'good bye,' they severally took their departure.

BY THE SAME AUTHOR.

Price 7s. 6d.

THE RIGHTS AND LIBERTIES OF THE CHURCH.

"There is so much that is right-minded in his book, so much real thoughtfulness, so much true observation, good information, and general sound sense, that we are compelled to speak on the one or two cases where we are obliged to differ, rather than on the many where we go with him heart and soul. Especially we would touch upon his remarks on Mr. Gladstone's view of Church and State, as showing his capacity as a critic. It is only fair to say that we have never seen more sagacious and acute remarks on that much discussed volume."—LITERARY CHURCHMAN.

"This volume appears at a very opportune period, and is destined, we believe, to exercise an important influence in the contest for the defence of the Church that must inevitably take place."—CHURCH TIMES.

Price 3s.

THE REFORMATION IN IRELAND AND THE SUBSEQUENT HISTORY OF ITS CHURCH.

"We heartily wish that this compendious little history had come out two years ago, and had been widely circulated and carefully read before the Parliamentary discussions on Ireland began. . . . Though short it is by no means dry or barren, and it gives the salient points of the history in a style which fixes the attention and convinces the judgment."—RECORD.

W. SKEFFINGTON, 163, PICCADILLY, LONDON.

Second Thousand. Price 2s. 6d.

A CATECHISM ON GOSPEL HISTORY,

For Church Schools and Families.

Price 6d.

THE SIGNS OF THE TIMES:

A Sermon on the Social and Moral Condition of the Country.

A Cheap Edition for Distribution, 3s. 6d. per dozen.

"Well would it be were every pulpit in this distracted country occupied by such outspoken preachers."—HAMPSHIRE ADVERTISER.

RIVINGTONS, LONDON. HARRISON, LEEDS.

www.ingramcontent.com/pod-product-compliance
Lightning Source LLC
Chambersburg PA
CBHW020808230426

43666CB00007B/905